Table of Contents

Introduction

James Maurice Gavin was born in 1907 and raised by adoptive parents in Pennsylvania.[1] He enlisted in 1924 at the age of 17 and served one year in Panama with the Coastal Artillery Corps before entering the United States Military Academy at West Point in 1925.[2] Gavin was commissioned in the infantry in 1929 and, intrigued by the promise of air power, attended the Air Corps Flying School but failed to earn his pilot's wings. He returned to the infantry and served in various units in around the United States and in the Philippines.[3] After company command, he returned to West Point as a tactics instructor for one year from 1940-1941 where he studied the rapid German victories in Europe.[4] Gavin recognized the promise of airborne operations and volunteered for parachute training in 1941.[5] He served as a company commander and operations officer in the new parachute organization before he assumed command of the 505th Parachute Infantry Regiment in 1942.[6]

Gavin entered World War II in the North Africa theater, his 505th PIR assigned to Ridgway's 82nd Airborne Division as of March 1943.[7] Ridgway selected the 505th as the sole American airborne regiment for the invasion of Sicily, and Gavin's first combat jump came in July 1943.[8] Gavin gained valuable experience in Sicily; he notably recognized the need for improved antitank weapons and pathfinders to mark drop zones for the paratroopers.[9] Gavin saw combat again in September 1943 when the 82nd jumped

---

[1] T. Michael Booth and Duncan Spencer, *Paratrooper: The Life of General James M. Gavin* (New York: Simon & Schuster, 1994), 19-22.

[2] Bradley Biggs, *Gavin* (Hamden, CT: Archon Books, 1980), 19-23.

[3] Ibid., 25-26.

[4] Booth and Spencer, *Paratrooper*, 64-65.

[5] Biggs, *Gavin*, 28-29.

[6] Ibid., 29-30.

[7] Booth and Spencer, *Paratrooper*, 85.

[8] Ibid., 86, 91, 96.

[9] James M. Gavin, *On to Berlin: Battles of an Airborne Commander 1943-1946* (New York: Viking Press, 1978), 51-52. See also Booth and Spencer, *Paratrooper*, 120.

into Salerno, Italy.[10] Ridgway promoted him to Brigadier General and made him the Assistant Division Commander in Naples on October 10, 1943.[11] As ADC, Gavin's first task was to serve as the airborne planner for the invasion of Normandy, a position he held until jumping into Normandy in command of the 82nd's parachute regiments on June 6, 1944.[12] Gavin served as ADC until August 16, 1944 when Ridgway assumed command of XVIII Airborne Corps and Gavin took command of the 82nd.[13] Gavin's first action as division commander was his fourth combat jump, into Nijmegen, Holland on September 17, 1944, during the ill-fated Operation Market-Garden.[14] With his promotion to Major General on October 20, 1944, he was the youngest Major General since George Armstrong Custer.[15] Gavin's next call came when the 82nd was in reserve in France. The German offensive in the Ardennes Forest in December 1944 started the Battle of the Bulge, and Gavin, briefly the acting XVIII Airborne Corps Commander, entered the battle with the 82nd taking positions around Werbomont and the 101st defending in Bastogne.[16] As the 82nd fought on towards Berlin through spring 1945, Gavin encountered the Woebblin Concentration Camp and forced the German citizens to bury the bodies of the dead.[17] In August 1945, Ridgway selected the 82nd for occupation duty in Berlin where Gavin stayed until he redeployed home from the war in December 1945.[18] With four combat jumps and over two years of fighting through Sicily, Italy, Normandy, Holland, France, and Germany, Major General James Gavin returned to the United States as one of the most highly regarded generals in the war.

---

[10] Booth and Spencer, *Paratrooper*, 137.

[11] Ibid., 144.

[12] Gavin, *On to Berlin*, 100.

[13] Ibid., 142-143.

[14] Booth and Spencer, *Paratrooper*, 214.

[15] Ibid., 212.

[16] Ibid., 249-252.

[17] Ibid., 292-295.

[18] Ibid., 300, 312.

After the war, Gavin remained in command of the 82nd Airborne Division until March 1948 when he left Fort Bragg and took over as Chief of Staff, Fifth Army.[19] Having served in Fifth Army for less than a year, Gavin worked on the Army Staff in the Pentagon with special duty on the Weapons System Evaluation Group, a weapons development team that consisted of a mix of military officers and scientists who worked on various systems for the atomic age.[20] In June 1951, Gavin received orders to Italy to serve as Chief of Staff in NATO Southern Command, a position he held until he assumed command of VII Corps in Germany in December 1952.[21] He commanded VII Corps until 1954 when he returned to the Pentagon to serve the new Army Chief of Staff, General Ridgway, as Assistant Chief of Staff for Operations (Department of the Army G-3).[22] Gavin received his promotion to lieutenant general in March 1955 and retired in 1958 over disagreements with defense policy.[23] After retirement, Gavin worked for a research and consulting firm, Arthur D. Little, Inc. and rose quickly to lead the company.[24] Gavin developed a friendship with a rising political figure in the late 1950s, John F. Kennedy, who agreed with many of Gavin's thoughts about defense policy.[25] When Kennedy won the 1960 election, he selected Gavin as his ambassador to France, a position Gavin held in 1960 and 1961.[26] Gavin returned to Arthur D. Little, Inc. but remained a commentator on defense policy and foreign affairs, including several congressional hearings regarding the Vietnam War in the late 1960s.[27] James M. Gavin died on February 23, 1990.[28]

---

[19] Guy A. Lofaro, *Encyclopedia of World War II: A Political, Social, and Military History*, Vol. 2: D-K, ed. Spencer C. Tucker, (Santa Barbara, CA: ABC-Clio, 2005), s.v. "Gavin, James Maurice."

[20] Biggs, *Gavin*, 74-75 and Booth and Spencer, *Paratrooper*, 322-329.

[21] Biggs, *Gavin*, 78 and Booth and Spencer, *Paratrooper*, 341.

[22] Booth and Spencer, *Paratrooper*, 344-347.

[23] Lofaro, "Gavin, James Maurice," 572.

[24] Biggs, *Gavin*, 106-113.

[25] Booth and Spencer, *Paratrooper*, 397-402.

[26] Lofaro, "Gavin, James Maurice," 572.

[27] Booth and Spencer, *Paratrooper*, 421-431.

[28] Lofaro, "Gavin, James Maurice," 572.

In all, Lieutenant General James Gavin was an experienced and revered wartime commander and intellectual officer struggling to equip and reorganize the army for future conflict within the constraints of budget and politics. His outspoken concepts and criticism give a window into the challenges he and his contemporaries faced while fighting to preserve and reshape the army. As he wrote in 1947, "never in the history of mankind, certainly, has anything affected man's thinking and his probably military behavior so drastically as the atomic bomb. It changes – must greatly change – our whole military thinking, organization, and tactics."[29] The direction for change, in light of the emergence of atomic weapons, defined a generation of leaders in the army following World War II and the Korean War. Gavin was on the forefront of those discussions and was outspoken in his disagreement with policy decisions of the day.

Historians have focused on a select few of Gavin's post-WWII contributions to military thought and practice, but a focused study of his concepts compared against actual changes in military organizations and doctrine has not emerged. Gavin had foresight of the challenges of future conflicts and influenced thinking within the army about how to organize, equip, and fight those conflicts. His ideas were not always popular or realized in actual conflicts, but he nonetheless set concepts in motion that shaped military thought and organizations that continued through the Cold War.

Based on confrontation with a complex and changing world, General Gavin developed and refined ideas on the methods and organization for future warfare. He developed a theory about the possible form of future warfare and advocated the need for the Army to have the flexibility and capability to fight in atomic and non-atomic wars of general and limited variety. Gavin consistently used three concepts he saw as central to dual-role capability that organized his approach to research and development and modernization. Those unifying concepts were mobility, firepower, and control. He greatly influenced the development of air mobility, tactical nuclear weapons, and organizational modernization as he struggled to reshape the army to fight limited wars in response to the Soviet threats in Europe and around the world. Gavin's frustration with policy decisions and Washington politics led to his

[29] James M. Gavin, *Airborne Warfare* (Washington, DC: Infantry Journal Press, 1947), 140.

4

retirement, but his search for solutions in his uncertain environment may inform current officers about how to consider and address the role, form, and function of military forces in times of uncertainty.

Only two biographies of LTG Gavin exist, *Paratrooper* (1994) by T. Michael Booth and Duncan Spencer and *Gavin* (1980) by Bradley Biggs. General Gavin's papers at the U.S. Army Military History Institute contain an unpublished autobiographical work that formed much of the basis for Booth and Spencer's book. *Paratrooper* focuses on Gavin's early life and World War II experience but also devotes significant effort to his post-WWII life and career, especially his losing battles in Washington.[30] Booth and Spencer do not specifically evaluate his theories and their implementation as much as his conflicts with military and political leaders that led to his retirement in 1958. Biggs, on the other hand, limits discussion of Gavin's early life and military career to two chapters of his book and devotes the rest of his effort to Gavin's outspoken post-war career where he was often at odds with national policies and higher-ranking officers in the Pentagon.[31] Biggs centered his work on a series of interviews with General Gavin in the 1960s and 1970s and told the story of Gavin's efforts to modernize the army, improve mobility, and argue for the relevance of conventional military land power despite the political reliance on strategic atomic weapons.

In 1967 Russell Weigley published his *History of the United States Army* that outlines the history of both the Regular Army and the citizen soldiers of the National Guard, Army Reserve, draftees and various militias. He updated the book in 1984 with a chapter covering the Vietnam conflict and the Cold War army in Europe. Weigley's broad subject matter precludes a detailed look at specific influential officers, but he does note Gavin as one of three senior generals (Ridgway and Taylor as the other two) that resigned out of frustrations over policy during the Eisenhower administration that "neglected

---

[30] Michael T. Booth and Duncan Spencer, *Paratrooper: The Life of Gen. James M. Gavin* (New York, NY: Simon & Schuster, 1994), 18.

[31] Bradley Biggs, *Gavin* (Hamden, CT: Archon Books, 1980), 8.

conventional forms of military power and relied unduly upon nuclear bombs."[32] Owing to the scope of his

book, Weigley's analysis of the evolution of military organizations focuses more on strategic and policy

decisions than individuals developing and implementing concepts for future conflict. However, when

discussing post-Korean War changes in the army and criticism of the intellectual qualities of military

schools and the officer corps, he specifically noted Gavin, Ridgway, and Taylor as examples of

intellectually stimulated officers who offered "broad and constructive thought" that helped shape national

security policy.[33] Weigley also devoted a chapter of his 1973 book, *The American Way of War: A History

of United States Military Strategy and Policy*, to "Strategy Intellectuals" in which he discussed Gavin's

War and Peace in the Space Age as a "sweeping indictment" of Eisenhower's "persisting inflexibilities

and budgetary limitations."[34] He also noted Gavin's emphasis on mobility, both strategic long-range and

tactical short-range airlift, required to rapidly exploit opportunities in future limited war.[35] Weigley

clearly considered Gavin as a strategic intellectual, but it would be outside the scope of his work to follow

the impact of a single officer's work.

Numerous authors discussed the emergence of air mobility in the Army. Several books recognize

Gavin as an early advocate of air mobility concepts and identify specific articles he wrote as having made

an impact on promoting air cavalry.[36] Frederic Bergerson, Stephen Rosen, Jacob Stockfisch, John Tolson,

---

[32] Russell Frank Weigley, *History of the United States Army* (Bloomington, IN: Indiana University Press, 1984), 526.

[33] Ibid., 553.

[34] Russell Frank Weigley, *The American Way of War: A History of United States Military Strategy and Policy* (Bloomington, IN: Indiana University Press, 1977), 422.

[35] Ibid., 423-424.

[36] Among the books that cover air mobility are the following: Frederic A. Bergerson, *The Army Gets an Air Force: Tactics of Insurgent Bureaucratic Politics* (Baltimore, MD: Johns Hopkins University Press, 1980); Christopher C.S. Cheng, *Air Mobility: The Development of a Doctrine* (Westport, CT: Praeger Publishers, 1994); John R. Galvin, *Air Assault: The Development of Airmobile Warfare* (New York: Hawthorn Books, 1969); Thomas G. Mahnken, *Technology and the American Way of War* (New York: Columbia University Press, 2008); Stephen Peter Rosen, *Winning the Next War: Innovation and the Modern Military* (Ithaca, NY: Cornell University Press, 1991); Jacob A. Stockfish, *The 1962 Howze Board and Army Combat Developments* (Santa Monica, CA: RAND, 1994); John J. Tolson, *Airmobility 1961-1971*, Department of the Army Vietnam Studies Series (Washington, DC: Government Printing Office, 1973); and Richard P. Weinert, Jr., *A History of Army Aviation – 1950-1962*, TRADOC Historical Monograph Series (Fort Monroe, VA: U.S. Army Training and Doctrine Command, 1991).

and Richard Weinert also noted specific instances where Gavin either selected individuals for key positions that influenced aviation development or tasked his staff to consider tactical use of air vehicles. However, none of the books focus specifically on Gavin's contribution to the theory and implementation of air mobility over time.

Robert Doughty discussed the evolution of U.S. Army tactical doctrine in his 1979 paper, *The Evolution of US Army Tactical Doctrine: 1946-1976*. He described Gavin's concepts regarding employment and mitigation of tactical atomic weapons and recommendations for organizing the army to operate in both atomic and non-atomic warfare.[37] Doughty also credited Gavin's advocacy of helicopter-borne cavalry with forming the "conceptual basis for doctrinal development of the helicopter in the 1950s."[38]

A.J. Bacevich's 1986 history of the post-Korean U.S. Army of the 1950s, *The Pentomic Era* identified the problem facing army officers of the era. "New technology, changing views of the nature of war, and the fiscal principles of the Eisenhower administration produced widespread doubts about the utility of traditional land forces."[39] Bacevich evaluated the army's changes during the 1950s in response to this problem. He specifically noted Gavin's position as the Deputy Chief of Staff for Research and Development, his public criticism of Eisenhower's reliance on atomic weapons and his advocacy of a flexible, mobile, and sizable force to respond to the threat of Soviet expansion.[40] Bacevich detailed the factors driving reorganization of WWII-style divisions to the Pentomic concept, and though Gavin is prominently featured in his analysis, a detailed look at his writing and influence is outside the scope of his topic.

---

[37] Robert A. Doughty, *The Evolution of US Army Tactical Doctrine: 1946-1976* (Fort Leavenworth, KS: Combat Studies Institute Press, 1979), 13, 16.

[38] Doughty, 27.

[39] A. J. Bacevich, *The Pentomic Era* (Washington, DC: National Defense University Press, 1986), 3.

[40] Ibid., 42-43.

John B. Wilson wrote *Maneuver and Firepower: The Evolution of Divisions and Separate Brigades* in 1998 as part of the Army Lineage Series for the U.S. Army Center of Military History. His extensive work documents the various reorganizations as the army sought to build the most effective combined arms teams.[41] Throughout the work, Wilson discusses the emergence and evolution of airborne and airmobile units, but does not specifically refer to Gavin's influence on either organization.

Paul Jussel, in his 2004 PhD dissertation, "Intimidating the World: The United States Atomic Army, 1956-1960," notes Gavin as one of the generals, along with Taylor and Ridgway, that fought against Eisenhower's New Look policy. They were looking to "balance the obvious benefits of nuclear weapons with an army organized and equipped to counter the nation's threats."[42] Jussel discussed Gavin's priorities for reorganization following his command in Europe to address dispersion, communications, and mobility when designing forces for the atomic battlefield.[43] He also identified Gavin as one of the uniquely qualified senior officers to comment on atomic weapons and missiles based on his experience with the Weapons System Evaluation Group.[44] However, Jussel's work is bound to a short window of time and consideration of Gavin's theories in light of organizational changes, his response to the Pentomic reorganization, or the development of air mobility are outside the scope of his thesis.

Ingo Trauschweitzer's *The Cold War U.S. Army: Building Deterrence for Limited War* (2008) is a history covering doctrine, strategy, planning, organizational structure, and technology.[45] He considers the army's cognitive problem following the emergence of the atomic bomb and the decades of transformations and reorganizations which sought to answer budget and policy limitations while building

---

[41] John B. Wilson, *Maneuver and Firepower: The Evolution of Divisions and Separate Brigades* (Washington, DC: Center of Military History, United States Army, 1998), vii-viii.

[42] Paul C. Jussel, "Intimidating the World: The United States Atomic Army, 1956-1960" (PhD diss., The Ohio State University, 2004), 24.

[43] Ibid., 39-40, 177.

[44] Ibid., 41.

[45] Ingo Trauschweizer, *The Cold War U.S. Army: Building Deterrence for Limited War* (Lawrence, KS: University Press of Kansas, 2008), 1.

a force capable of fighting the Soviet threat in Europe. Trauschweizer covers Gavin's evaluation of atomic battlefield tactics with VII Corps in the early 1950s that he partially credits with envisioning the dispersed "battle-group" later subsumed by the Pentomic Division concept.[46] He also discusses Gavin's advocacy for air mobility in the 1950s. Trauschweizer's history of the Cold War army notes Gavin in the roles with which he is typically associated, but is not concerned with a comparison of Gavin's theories with the specific changes encountered in the army.

Published in 2008, Robert Davis II considered post-conflict army changes in *The Challenge of Adaptation: The US Army in the Aftermath of Conflict, 1953-2000*. He reviewed the army's adaptations based on limitations and concepts of future conflict after the Korean War, the Vietnam War, and the Cold War using doctrine, divisional organizations, training and education.[47] Davis noted Gavin's alliance with Ridgway in opposition to Eisenhower's defense policies.[48] Davis also discussed the VII Corps exercises where Gavin tested the need for dispersion, communications, air mobility, and tactical nuclear weapons.[49] Although Davis discussed airmobile development, he did not mention Gavin's role in influencing its acceptance. Davis described post-conflict change, but Gavin's concept of future warfare or his concepts to prepare the army for that future war are outside the scope of his work.

Section one discusses Gavin's primary works. Starting with *Airborne Warfare*, published in 1947, he wrote extensively about his World War II experience in the 82nd Airborne Division and included three chapters about future airborne armies, anti-airborne defense, and the future employment of airborne forces. As early as 1947 he wrote about the "interesting possibilities" offered by helicopters.[50] General Gavin refined his thoughts on mobility, integration of tactical nuclear weapons, and optimal organizations

---

[46] Ibid., 49.

[47] Robert T. Davis II, *The Challenge of Adaptation: The US Army in the Aftermath of Conflict, 1953-2000* (Fort Leavenworth, KS: Combat Studies Institute Press, 2008), 2.

[48] Ibid., 19-20.

[49] Ibid., 25.

[50] Gavin, *Airborne Warfare*, 151.

for limited warfare in several articles during the 1950s.[51] Shortly after his retirement in 1958, Gavin published *War and Peace in the Space Age*, which refined a number of his concepts that he first published as articles and outlined the circumstances that pushed him to retirement. In this book, Gavin advocated "specific recommendations in the related fields of tactics, strategy, and organization."[52] Gavin's consistent themes throughout his works include his theory of the form of future warfare, the need for dual-role readiness, and the concepts of mobility, firepower, and control needed for effectiveness on the future battlefield.

Section two evaluates specific organizational concepts that Gavin envisioned to fight in either atomic or non-atomic war. It starts with his immediate post-WWII look at reorganization of airborne divisions. Section two continues with Gavin's refined idea on the type of war he expected to face based on his understanding of the Soviet threat and communist actions in Korea and Indochina. Section two closes by reviewing his concepts for air mobile cavalry and wider division-level reorganization principles.

Section three examines Gavin's influence on actual reorganization and modernization efforts up to Vietnam. This section considers Gavin's concepts as they manifested in the pentomic divisions and his response to that reorganization effort implemented in the mid-1950s under General Taylor. Next, it covers Gavin's influence on the development and adoption of air mobile units through his promotion of the concept and his placement of key individuals to advance the idea. Lastly, the section discusses the influential Howze Board and how Gavin's influence manifested in the board's recommendations that led to the formation of airmobile units in the Army in the mid-1960s.

General Gavin developed a theory of future warfare that he used to refine his concepts for functions, organizations, and technology for future conflicts. His vision of an army with dual capability

---

[51] A sampling of Gavin's articles relevant to this study includes the following: "The Future of Airborne Operations" (1947), "The Future of Armor" (1948), "The Tactical Use of the Atomic Bomb" (1950), "Cavalry, and I Don't Mean Horses" (1954), "New Divisional Organizations" (1955), "Arms Vigilance for Peace" (1955), "We Can Solve Our Technical Difficulties" (1955), and "The Mobility Differential" (1963).

[52] James M. Gavin, *War and Peace in the Space Age* (New York, NY: Harper & Brothers, 1958), 2.

for atomic- and non-atomic warfare, in limited or general war, organized his approach to research and development for and modernization of the army following World War II and during the early Cold War. His concepts of mobility, firepower, and control were common through most of his writing. Gavin had a significant impact on tactical nuclear weapons, missiles, air mobility, and organizational transformation as his generation of officers sought to ensure the Army's relevance in and readiness for future warfare.

Section 1: Why He Wrote – Gavin's Vision of Future Conflict

Gavin published *Airborne Warfare* in 1947 to document the refinement of airborne combat during World War II and consider future development and employment of airborne forces in light of the emergence of atomic weapons.[53] In this book, he outlined in detail the airborne operations in Sicily, Italy, Normandy, Holland, Corregidor, and Germany. Writing about the jump into Salerno, he noted:

> The airborne troops had a decisive influence on the final outcome of the Salerno operation as a whole. At a moment when the scales of defeat and victory were in balance, the weight of the airborne reserves tipped them to the side of victory. … The airborne troops had a mobility and striking power that no high commander could overlook in the future. Correct and timely commitment and exploitation of such forces could turn the tide of battle.[54]

While he recognized the advantage of airborne employment, Gavin also clearly outlined the vulnerability of paratroopers facing mobile, armored opponents and the inherent isolation they faced once dropped into enemy territory. Considering those vulnerabilities, he considered the best missions for airborne forces as seizing key terrain, blocking movement of enemy reserves, rapid reinforcement, and cutting enemy lines of communication.[55] Using the Normandy invasion as evidence, Gavin described the successful employment of airborne troops against those types of missions to exploit the "great advantage of initiative" of airborne forces in relation to defenders.[56] With his background in development of the

---

[53] Gavin, *Airborne Warfare*, 140.

[54] Ibid., 31.

[55] Ibid., 35.

[56] Ibid., 67.

airborne concept and his experience in World War II, Gavin thus considered how to maintain the advantage that airborne forces provided to a commander.

Not content with describing the last war, Gavin envisioned movement through the air as the most important means for waging future war. In his words, "only by exploiting to its utmost the great potential of flight can we combine complete dispersion in the defense with the facility of rapidly massing for counterattack which today's and tomorrow's Army must possess."[57] He considered airborne troops strategically necessary for offensive and defensive conflicts in order to seize key airheads and atomic production and delivery systems to build friendly combat power or prevent their use by enemy forces.[58] After explaining the need for airborne troops, he described the development of the tools of airborne warfare (the parachute, glider, and transport plane) and his vision of where future technical development should focus.[59] Gavin included improved anti-tank weapons, tactical vehicles, and radios in his discussion of research and development needs.[60] He also envisioned future employment of airborne divisions, corps, and armies, and outlined how an airhead seizure might progress, emphasizing the speed and initiative necessary to succeed.[61] To complete his comprehensive look at airborne warfare, Gavin reviewed division-level organizations from the World Wars and proposed a future division organization adaptable to combat on the atomic battlefield.[62] Gavin's discussion of the ways and means of future warfare demonstrated his ability to synthesize his experience with his prediction of the nature of atomic warfare.

General Gavin followed *Airborne Warfare* with a series of articles for both military and popular audiences. In December 1947, he wrote "The Future of Airborne Operations," published in *Military Review*. Gavin argued that airpower focused on bombers was not going to be the decisive arm of airpower

---

[57] Ibid., 140.

[58] Ibid., 141.

[59] Ibid., 142-151.

[60] Ibid., 151, 159, 175.

[61] Ibid., 154-157.

[62] Ibid., 163-166.

because missiles could replace bombers in the strategic bombing role.[63] Rather, he anticipated that the air delivery of ground combat power would be decisive in future combat.[64] To advocate development of specialized air vehicles for future combat, Gavin compared aircraft development to that of sea craft that were purpose-built for specific tasks during amphibious operations.[65] His stated that, "to assume that the ordinary small commercial airplane can survive the spewing sea of flak that comes up from the modern battlefield is to assume that any ordinary small commercial boat could have been used to assault Utah and Omaha beaches."[66] Gavin felt that research, development, and procurement funding focused on heavy bombers and missiles ignored the decisive role that he envisioned airmobile ground forces playing in future conflict.

Continuing his theme of air-delivered ground combat power, Gavin wrote "The Future of Armor" for *Infantry Journal* in January 1948. In this article, he contended that light air-transportable tanks must replace heavy tanks and he continued his advocacy for development of aircraft for tactical mobility.[67] Gavin introduced his concept of airborne armored cavalry in this article. In his words, "striking at high speed by air, and entering ground combat that requires mobility and the retention of the initiative until the decision is gained, the armored cavalry will play the decisive role in future airborne combat."[68] He considered the leadership traits of "boldness, aggressiveness, flexibility of mind and mental as well as physical courage" that were traditionally associated with cavalry were critical for airborne combat.[69] He reviewed several fellow officers' views on the need for air-transportable armor and discussed the

---

[63] James M. Gavin, "The Future of Airborne Operations," *Military Review* 27, no. 9 (December 1947): 3-4.

[64] Ibid., 4-5.

[65] Ibid., 5-6.

[66] Ibid., 7.

[67] James M. Gavin, "The Future of Armor," *Infantry Journal* 62, no. 1 (January 1948): 7.

[68] Gavin, "The Future of Armor," 11.

[69] Ibid., 7.

requirement for the strategic mobility of armor to match the strategic mobility of the troops it supports.[70]

He then described the historic pattern of firepower and mobility exchanging dominance over time, suggesting that light armored vehicles with "highly penetrative guns" may replace the heavy tank.[71] Gavin again used the historic parallel of sea power development with that of air power to explain his argument that America must continue innovation of air power to move armored divisions, employing lighter, more mobile vehicles, strategically and tactically by air.[72] In this article, Gavin argued against the trend towards increasingly heavy tanks while continuing to advocate for air-delivered combat power.

As he considered the situation unfolding on the Korean Peninsula in the summer and fall of 1950, Gavin wrote "The Tactical Use of the Atomic Bomb" in November 1950. This article represented a shift in Gavin's focus on air mobility but demonstrated development of his thoughts regarding the emergence of atomic weapons. Gavin's role in weapons development with the Weapons System Evaluation Group in 1949 best explains his sudden emergence as a military expert on atomic weapons.[73] He argued that the commonly held belief that atomic bombs would decisively end a war by employment "against the economy and the noncombatant elements of a nation's population" was misguided.[74] He felt that atomic weapons represented a useful tactical option and used several examples in World War II, specifically Normandy, Iwo Jima, and Okinawa, where atomic weapons could have been useful.[75] Without claiming that tactical use of atomic bombs would end the war, he suggested that they would "contribute greatly to the common battle achievement" if employed "whenever it is possible to deliver it profitably."[76] When reprinting this article in 1951, the editors of the *Bulletin of the Atomic Scientists* considered Gavin the

---

[70] Gavin, "The Future of Armor," 8.

[71] Ibid., 8-9.

[72] Ibid., 10-11.

[73] Booth and Spencer, 327-329.

[74] James M. Gavin, "The Tactical Use of the Atomic Bomb," *Combat Forces Journal* 1, no. 4 (November 1950): 9.

[75] Ibid., 9-10.

[76] Ibid., 11.

only "prominent military expert" openly considering atomic weapons in a tactical role instead of in the strategic role normally associated with atomic bombs.[77] While Gavin's shift in focus to firepower in the form of atomic weapons instead of air mobility was a result of his posting to the Weapons System Evaluation Group, it demonstrated his ability to envision future uses for current and emerging technologies.

In one of his most widely referenced articles, Gavin wrote for a popular audience but returned to his primary theme, air mobility, but now included trends in atomic firepower. Published by *Harper's Magazine* in 1954, "Cavalry, and I Don't Mean Horses" represented Gavin's public commentary on the shortfalls of defense spending priorities and laments the stalemate in Korea. He argued that General Walker's Eighth Army was missing a vital element of combat power by not having air-mobile cavalry to screen in front of his forces and exploit opportunities presented.[78] Gavin introduced the concept of a "mobility differential" in this article, the idea that cavalry requires greater mobility than the forces it supports.[79] He returned to his argument from "The Future of Armor" that heavy tanks could not serve a cavalry role since they were no faster than motorized infantry were. Gavin felt that a true cavalry arm could deny the enemy surprise and return the advantage of surprise to the U.S. Army in both a Korean-style conflict or against the Soviet threat in Europe.[80] Reflecting on maneuvers with VII Corps in Europe, Gavin wrote, "All the soul-searching in the world, and the most brilliant staff cerebrations, will not conjure up tactical success in cavalry action unless the means of achieving it are provided our cavalry commanders. They do not have the means today."[81] He argued that the means required included mobility,

---

[77] Editor's commentary preceding James M. Gavin, "The Tactical Use of the Atomic Bomb," *Bulletin of the Atomic Scientists* 7, no. 2, (February 1951): 46. In this same issue, Dr. J. Robert Oppenheimer also wrote about the possible tactical use of atomic bombs while suggesting that their deterrent value may be their most decisive attribute.

[78] James M. Gavin, "Cavalry, and I Don't Mean Horses," *Harper's Magazine*, April 1954, 54-55.

[79] Ibid., 54.

[80] Ibid., 54-55.

[81] Ibid., 56.

which the "aerial instrument" offered, but mobility was more than speed, it was the capability to deliver superior firepower.[82] Gavin closed the article with a return to the primary defense question of the day, the atomic bomb. He explained that defense against the bomb required great dispersion in the defense and mobility, through the air, to mutually support over great distance and concentrate rapidly to gain momentum for decisive battle.[83] While "Cavalry, and I Don't Mean Horses" marked Gavin's return to advocating greater air mobility, he clearly felt that national policy established misdirected funding priorities for research, development, and equipping the army.

Gavin returned to addressing a primarily military audience as he discussed organizing a force for fighting in atomic or non-atomic war. The Army was testing new structures to fill that dual-role, though Gavin expected that the most likely type of conflict was the "non-atomic peripheral war."[84] He emphasized control of the reorganized force and outlined "combat commands" and "battle groups" that replaced regiments and battalions, with the new units designed for deployment in a "cellular rather than linear" fashion.[85] Gavin also described the new units as "taking advantage of every new development in communications, intelligence gathering, firepower, and above all mobility" to enable dispersed operations and rapid concentration required on future battlefields.[86] In this discussion, Gavin succinctly highlighted the need for mobility, firepower, and control while he discussed the Army's attempts to reorganize for war on a nuclear battlefield.

In a March 1955 interview for *The Army Combat Forces Journal* with Theodore White, Gavin continued his discussion of ongoing reorganization efforts and framed his anticipated form of future warfare. Gavin described that the problem facing Army leaders was "to find the optimum density over the

---

[82] Ibid., 58.

[83] Ibid., 60.

[84] "New Divisional Organizations," *Army-Navy-Air Force Register* 76, no. 3923 (February 12, 1955): 1. The article is an account of a news conference Gavin gave to discuss ongoing exercises that were testing reorganized division structures based on the Chief of Staff of the Army, General Ridgway's, guidance.

[85] Ibid., 1.

[86] Ibid., 1, 21.

optimum depth – enough to hold the enemy on the ground … until you organize help and reinforcement for a counterblow."[87] He discussed the dispersion of a division expanding from a "front of ten to fifteen miles … [with] a depth of five miles" to a front of 30 miles and depth up to 125 miles because a concentrated force offered a lucrative target for enemy tactical atomic weapons.[88] To fight in this environment, Gavin argued that the Army needed air mobility to deliver forces quickly and sustain them once isolated.[89] To achieve the required tactical and strategic mobility, for combat and logistics, he returned to his parallel with amphibious warfare and recommended that the Army develop specialized air vehicles much like the Navy built amphibious sea vehicles for specific tactical tasks in warfare.[90] He suggested area rather than linear control and that the Army was "working on the problem [of controlled dispersion] intensively, both theoretically and in the field."[91] Forthcoming communications systems were to enable such control.[92] This interview continued Gavin's advocacy for air mobility, dual-role (atomic and non-atomic) forces, and further described the challenges he expected in future warfare, not least was control of dispersed forces.

Gavin expanded his audience to include industrial partners with an article in the March-April 1955 issue of *Ordnance* magazine. In this article, he clearly supported the Eisenhower administration's desire to support healthy economic growth, but focused on "maintaining common enterprise with our allies and … sufficient military strength to win any war that may be forced on us."[93] He outlined the United States' strategic setting and the Soviet threat and offered multiple courses of action that could

---

[87] Theodore H. White, "An Interview with General Gavin … Tomorrow's Battlefield," *Army Combat Forces Journal* (March 1955): 20.

[88] Ibid., 21.

[89] Ibid.

[90] Ibid., 23.

[91] Ibid., 22.

[92] Ibid.

[93] James M. Gavin, "Arms Vigilance for Peace," *Ordnance* 39, no. 209 (March-April 1955): 718. Ingo Trauschweizer's book, *The Cold War U.S. Army*, is one of several books and authors that cover Eisenhower's defense policy and the challenges the Army faced during his tenure.

shape national military policy.[94] Gavin's recommended course was to "maintain flexible, versatile military strength able to cope with the variety of both defensive and offensive situations which might arise – such as cold wars, limited wars, wars of covert or overt aggression, general wars in which nuclear weapons were not used, or total wars utilizing weapons of every description."[95] In support of this course, Gavin outlined the firepower advancements made with the Army's development of tactical atomic weapons and missile technology and the vast expansion of the battlefield that such weapons necessitated.[96] Gavin stayed consistent with past writings in the remainder of the article and continued to advocate flexibility, tactical mobility, and improved communications and intelligence to enable control across the expanded battlefield.[97] Through multiple sources with varying audiences, Gavin advanced his concepts and sought to integrate them with national policy and Army traditionalists.

Gavin again considered national military policy and the Army's role with another article in November 1955. In "We Can Solve Our Technical Difficulties" he described the dual-functionality of the Army to "mobilize for large-scale war" and have "sizable forces in being, ready to move by land, sea, or air and fight any time, any place."[98] He categorized this ability to "move rapidly and put out 'brush fires' before they get out of control" as a credible deterrent to potential aggressors.[99] To provide this credible deterrent, he expressed confidence that the development of "mobility, firepower, organization, and combat readiness" for both functions was possible and within reach.[100] He felt that firepower, in the form of atomic artillery and missile technology, was adequate, but that "the decisive margin of strength will fall to the side possessing superior mobility to exploit the effects of weapons yielding greatly increased

_____

[94] Ibid., 716-718.

[95] Ibid., 718.

[96] Ibid., 718-719.

[97] Ibid., 719.

[98] James M. Gavin, "We Can Solve Our Technical Difficulties," *Army Combat Forces Journal* (November 1955): 64.

[99] Ibid.

[100] Ibid.

firepower."[101] Ground and air mobility vehicles needed further development, Gavin wrote, and the Army "should be capable of employing atomic firepower at the battle group level, of engaging and defeating a quantitatively superior enemy through superior tactical and logistics mobility, vastly increased firepower capability, control and command facilities."[102] He set up the Army as having the ability to use discriminating atomic power to defeat an enemy force without "destroying the foundations upon which a firm and lasting peace can be built at the cessation of hostilities."[103] With this article, Gavin continued to make the case for the Army's dual-role readiness, the need for mobility, firepower, and control, and against the over-reliance on strategic nuclear bombing.

Following his retirement in 1958, Gavin published his comprehensive book *War and Peace in the Space Age*. He sought to combine many of his observations into a book that considered all aspects of the problems he found with national defense and raise public awareness of defense issues in an effort to curtail the "menacing encroachment of Communism."[104] He offered a detailed explanation of his theory for future warfare and expanded his arguments about mobility, firepower, and control among a number of contextual historical, political, and strategic discussions. Gavin started with a description of the "missile lag," essentially a technology advantage that the Soviets enjoyed in the mid to late 1950s punctuated by the launch of the Sputnik satellite in 1957.[105] Gavin posited that missiles and satellites would make the entire world a tactical theater by 1965.[106] With the expanding tactical theater creating overlapping functions in land, sea, and air forces, he felt that the national defense organizations, the Department of Defense and Joint Chiefs of Staff, needed significant change to meet the problems of the next decades.[107]

---

[101] Ibid.

[102] Ibid., 65.

[103] Ibid.

[104] Gavin, *War and Peace in the Space Age*, ix-x.

[105] Ibid., 4-18.

[106] Ibid., 19.

[107] Ibid., 20.

Gavin's view of the direction of national defense and future warfare placed him at odds with senior military and political leaders.

To place his future concepts in context, Gavin discussed his work developing early airborne tactics and his experiences in World War II. He argued that focusing on the atomic bomb meant military professionals failed to learn the lessons of World War II despite their continuing relevance.[108] The first lesson was one of readiness. World War II demonstrated that America was slow to mobilize and ill equipped for combat.[109] Allied scientific prowess, which produced great strides in radar, rockets, communications, landing craft, and the atomic bomb, Gavin wrote, was one of the "truly great contributions to the Allied victory."[110] The second lesson, then, was the role that science played in maintaining a strategic advantage.[111] The final lesson was that each service contributed equally to victory, dispelling the popular interwar theory that air power alone could be decisive.[112] He considered the post-World War II obsession with the strategic bomber as the primary means of air power was misguided, that development of all forms of air power, to include improved transport aircraft for air mobility, was essential.[113] Gavin clearly felt that the United States military had failed to capitalize on the lessons of World War II and had paid the price in Korea.

Failing to learn the lessons of World War II was only part of the problem facing military planners at the time. The emergence of nuclear weapons and communist expansion each presented unique challenges; they became more problematic when considered as a whole. As mentioned in his article "The Tactical Use of the Atomic Bomb," Gavin's concept of using nuclear bombs in a tactical role was unpopular with the Air Force leadership, who preferred to retain control of nuclear material for strategic

---

[108] Ibid.

[109] Ibid., 93.

[110] Ibid., 95-96.

[111] Ibid., 96.

[112] Ibid., 96.

[113] Ibid., 103, 107.

use.[114] With regard to the situation in Korea, especially in the summer of 1950, he felt that it was "inexcusable to allow the 8th Army to be destroyed without even using the most powerful weapons in our arsenal."[115] Compounding the problems that nuclear weapons offered military planners was the increasing Soviet threat and Soviet beliefs that capitalism and communism could not coexist. He defined the problem facing military planners as trying to fulfill U.S. obligations to collective security agreements against the nuclear-armed Soviets while facing restrictive budget and personnel reductions under a defense spending policy that focused solely on nuclear retaliatory capability.[116] Unfortunately, the realities that military planners faced in Korea and Indochina did not conform to a model that warranted retaliatory nuclear response.

Gavin's work with the Weapons System Evaluation Group (WSEG) placed him in close contact with a number of highly talented scientists considering technical solutions for warfare. Gavin went to Korea in 1950 with a small team of scientists to look at the tactical problems facing the troops.[117] He noted the distinct lack of air support for the ground commanders and the recognized the need for improved communications and "firepower—probably missiles, and preferably nuclear—immediately responsible to him and under his control."[118] Project Vista grew out of this visit to Korea and was a joint "study of ground and air tactical warfare with particular attention to the defense of Western Europe in the immediate future."[119] Gavin considered Project Vista as a significant step towards improving the nation's ability to win limited wars.[120] Notable Project Vista recommendations to the Army included a lightweight tank killer (later developed by the Marine Corps), communications improvements, development of

---

[114] Ibid., 113-114.

[115] Ibid., 116.

[116] Ibid., 119-120.

[117] Ibid., 129.

[118] Ibid., 131.

[119] Ibid., 132.

[120] Ibid., 133.

tactical nuclear missiles, and improved intelligence systems.[121] Recommendations to the Air Force were largely in the realm of tactical support, in opposition to the prevalent strategic bomber focus. The concepts considered by the Vista scientists were largely in line with concepts that Gavin had written about in some fashion for several years. Undoubtedly, his influence with the scientists played a role in the team's recommendations and their work added to his understanding of the scientific possibilities.

In command of VII Corps in 1952, Gavin conducted wargames and field exercises to test his concepts for fighting on an atomic battlefield.[122] He looked closely at dispersion of the troops in defense and used expected weapons yields to select appropriate troop density in a given area.[123] He found that while the armored divisions were adequately organized, the infantry and cavalry organizations were inadequate to fight on the nuclear battlefield.[124] Not surprisingly, Gavin's first recommendation was to use helicopters to restore a "mobility differential" in the lead elements of the defense, the cavalry forces.[125] By increasing the dispersion of his troops, defensive depth greatly increased as well. Gavin's second recommendation was to replace artillery with mobile missiles, armed with nuclear warheads, which could range the vastly increased depth of the battlefield.[126] Command and control over increased distances also required communications upgrades, and Gavin recommended fielding greater communications capability to lower echelons of command and establishing alternate command posts out of range of a single nuclear blast.[127] With expanded distances and areas of responsibility, he saw air

---

[121] Ibid., 134-135. Gavin describes all the Project Vista recommendations on these two pages. Preceding paragraphs in the book discuss the controversy surrounding Dr. Oppenheimer's alleged use of Project Vista to suggest that Air Force doctrine for strategic bombing centered on the slaughter of civilians.

[122] Ibid., 136.

[123] Ibid., 136-137.

[124] Ibid., 137.

[125] Ibid.

[126] Ibid., 137-138.

[127] Ibid., 138.

mobility as the only logical solution for the expanded logistics problem.[128] From these observations and recommendations, Gavin refined his views on future combat and the optimal organizations to fight it.

Gavin's experience with NATO and VII Corps shaped his concepts as he returned to Washington, D.C. As Assistant Chief of Staff for Operations (G-3), he faced President Eisenhower's "New Look" defense policy that focused on massive nuclear retaliation and a reduction in conventional forces.[129] One of his primary struggles as G-3 was between this policy and his vision of future conflict and understanding of the necessary defense priorities to ensure the Army's readiness to fight in a nuclear- or non-nuclear environment. Gavin described his "immediate problem" as "whether or not in defending the Army budget before Congress, to agree to the basic philosophy of the New Look."[130] As he wrote,

> It meant agreeing to less emphasis upon the development of tactical nuclear weapons. It meant agreeing to close our minds once again to the challenges of tomorrow's land warfare, with the implied need for long-range missiles, improved radars and communications, VTOL and STOL air vehicles, and an increased Air Force Troop Carrier airlift. To disagree with the concept in testifying before Congress was to be insubordinate, and yet many of us were convinced that to agree would only once again advance our nation on the road to military disaster.[131]

The personnel end strength reduction concerned Gavin, but more problematic was the lack of funding for missile and satellite development that he viewed as critical to providing a tactical long-range firepower edge to the U.S. and its NATO allies.[132] His fundamental disagreement with the defense policy meant that he was either unable to argue for the research, development, and reorganization he felt was necessary to ensure the Army's readiness or insubordinate if he voiced his opinions to Congress.

Gavin claimed that, starting in 1955, the United States entered a decade in which it must fundamentally change defense policies in order to curtail the spread of communism. He argued, "Time is running out and we must … make the sacrifices necessary to create and maintain a military establishment

---

[128] Ibid.

[129] Ibid., 150.

[130] Ibid., 151.

[131] Ibid.

[132] Ibid., 153.

adequate to serve the needs of democracy."[133] To Gavin, this meant a capability to "apply power with

discrimination anywhere in the world, as the need arises, at any time."[134] He felt that a modern and

capable military sent a clear signal to Soviet aggressors that the West would respond immediately and it

would inspire confidence in fellow democratic nations. Deterrence, then, was not a function of strategic

nuclear power, but one of a capable standing military force able to respond immediately to aggression that

may not reach a level that warrants a strategic nuclear response. Gavin concluded, "We will either make

the necessary sacrifices to create the type of military establishment that can serve a positive, forward-

looking concept of democracy or we will succumb to the march of Communism."[135] With this political-

strategic perspective, Gavin sought to outline the type of military capability that could serve those

purposes.

Gavin started his description of military capability with a discussion of the basic essence of

warfare. He defined tactics as "the technique of employing the resources of war in battle."[136] Using that

starting point, he argued that the functions in war over time differ only in kind between a man, a "carrier

task force, a field army or a bomber wing."[137] He described,

> An effective weapons system must locate its target, transmit its behavior characteristics through a
> central communications system, set in motion the force available to destroy the target, follow
> with an evaluation of the results achieved, and prepare for the next action. In their simplest forms,
> these functions may be defined as a communications system, fire power and mobility.[138]

His description captures several concepts that he wrote extensively about and he noted that increasingly

complex systems required speed and automated computations to be effective.[139] Gavin argued that since

the functional elements of battle were consistent over time, with some foresight of future technology one

---

[133] Ibid., 206.

[134] Ibid.

[135] Ibid., 211.

[136] Ibid., 212.

[137] Ibid.

[138] Ibid.

[139] Ibid.

could "predict the future pattern that battles may take … [and] define with some accuracy the role of strategy."[140] With his description of the functions of war over time, Gavin sought to identify trends he saw and explain his vision of future warfare.

Gavin's vision of future warfare was one of war on a global scale. He considered the expansion of battlefield areas as a function of the range of weapons systems and the mobility of the forces involved.[141] Using his understanding of current and near-future weapons development, he saw warfare in the age of intercontinental ballistic missiles and long-range fighter-bombers as "involving the entire earth as a tactical theater."[142] Gavin also envisioned space-based assets, using satellites for reconnaissance, communications, weather study and prediction, and satellites and manned vehicles as weapons platforms unless a United Nations program could be established to control space operations.[143] Moving to the subject of future tactics, Gavin returned to one of his primary concepts, air mobility. He considered air-mobile forces armed with tactical nuclear weapons as "the key to the control of the land masses on this earth."[144] He imagined sky cavalry operating with "drone surveillance forces … the greatest innovation in tactical combat since the beginning of history."[145] Gavin clearly identified trends that the Army later exploited, even if his vision of earth as a tactical theater seems overstated when over fifty years after he wrote the United States still has the globe divided into geographic commands.

With the vision articulated above, Gavin more closely estimated the technical progress in firepower, mobility, and control mechanisms he expected to occur by 1965. With regard to firepower, he saw the availability of small-yield nuclear weapons to all military organizations as a critical requirement

---

[140] Ibid., 213.

[141] Ibid., 215-216.

[142] Ibid., 217.

[143] Ibid., 220-226.

[144] Ibid., 227-228.

[145] Ibid., 228.

for future limited wars.[146] He saw these small-yield weapons as useful for air defense, anti-armor defense, submarine (sea-land) and anti-submarine warfare while they also provided a supply advantage in that a given force would need fewer tactical nuclear weapons than the equivalent explosive amount of conventional munitions.[147] Paired with nuclear firepower advances, Gavin anticipated an "evolution" in mobility encompassing jet transports, small tactical air transports (if "properly exploited"), and sea mobility.[148] To control the firepower and mobility advances, he envisioned drone and satellite reconnaissance linked to a "highly responsive" series of computers as a communications system to enable target acquisition, control and engagement.[149] With these rapid advancements, Gavin felt that military organizations needed to adapt to meet the challenges introduced by employment of the new technology and suggested underlying principles for such reorganization.

In closing his comprehensive effort in *War and Peace in the Space Age*, Gavin advocated shifting from a "strategy to avoid war to a strategy for peace."[150] He felt that to limit national strategy to "a single strategy or tactic, and then announce it to the world, would be to surrender the initiative and thus to invite strategic failure and certain war."[151] This statement refers to the Eisenhower administration's focus on massive nuclear retaliation. Gavin felt that seizing the strategic initiative with a strategy for peace was possible, but required dedication and sacrifice from the American people and revised policies and research and development decisions from policy makers.[152] His position, and the resulting public turmoil within the national security arena, identified Gavin as an outsider at the highest military and political levels.

---

[146] Ibid., 265.

[147] Ibid., 265-266.

[148] Ibid., 266-267.

[149] Ibid., 268

[150] Ibid., 288.

[151] Ibid., 289.

[152] Ibid.

Gavin's focus did not drift from his core concepts of mobility, firepower, and control in his post-retirement writing. His 1963 article "The Mobility Differential" discussed the need and potential for innovation to gain greater mobility, which coupled with firepower and "reasonable intelligence and direction," resulted in more effective weapons systems.[153] Gavin advocated helicopters as an option to provide the mobility advantage that U.S. forces needed to fulfill the cavalry missions of "reconnaissance, screening, and exploitation."[154] He described several categories of air vehicles needed for reconnaissance, support, logistics, command and control, and unmanned reconnaissance, demonstrating the holistic approach to mobility he conceptualized.[155] Gavin's article reinforced his consistent concepts of mobility, firepower, and control with updated consideration for ongoing reorganization, research and development, and trends in the national defense policy that served to keep his views in the realm of public debate.

Section 2: Gavin's Concepts Applied to Organizational Structures

Based on his concepts of mobility, firepower, and control while considering the Soviet threat and the need for operations in a potentially nuclear war or a limited peripheral war, Gavin refined concepts for organizational structure that started with reorganization of airborne divisions, considered cavalry organizations, and evolved to a wider reorganization concept.

Before the Cold War dominated military policy and thought, Gavin considered future organization of an airborne division based on his concepts of mobility, firepower, and control derived from his experience in World War II. He described "the division of the future – and this division must be airborne or adaptable to air transport – must be thoroughly flexible. It must be readily able to fight in any direction in a defense, and to ward off blows from any direction while attacking. The division commander should be able to influence directly the action of any of his regiments."[156] Gavin's recommended division

---

[153] James M. Gavin, "The Mobility Differential," *Army* 13, no. 11 (June 1963): 34.

[154] Ibid., 34-35.

[155] Ibid., 36.

[156] Gavin, *Airborne Warfare*, 165.

(see figure one) contained four infantry regiments, two intermediate headquarters, division artillery, and unspecified combat support and service elements.

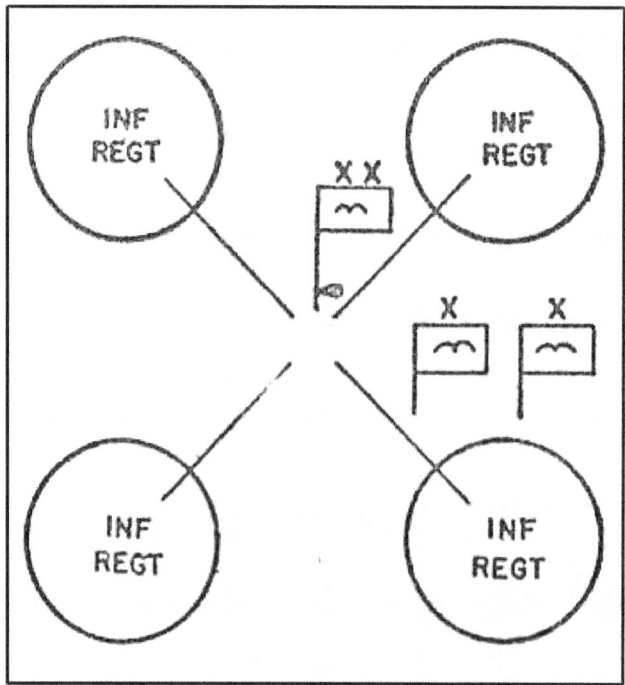

Figure 1: Gavin's Quadrilateral Division[157]

For mobility he stressed regiments limited to 2,400 infantrymen carrying lighter weight weapons with greater firepower than 1947 models. Mobility also included removing some combat service support units ("mobile showers, laundry units, refrigeration units, and the like") from the assault division and moving them to follow-on elements intended to fly in to a captured or improvised airfield complex "within a few weeks of the initial landings."[158] Despite recommending removal of service units from the airborne division to improve mobility, Gavin recognized the criticality of the supporting supply program. He outlined in detail the supporting engineering and supply elements required to follow the assaulting infantry but lamented that "so little [had] been done to develop airborne service units and special

---

[157] Gavin, *Airborne Warfare*, 164. Labeled "Figure I. Quadrilateral division of the future" in Gavin's original.

[158] Ibid., 166-167.

equipment for them. The army that solves these problems will be the army that wins."[159] To augment the firepower of the four infantry regiments, Gavin recommended organizing the division artillery (not pictured) with "four light battalions and one medium general support battalion."[160] To facilitate rapid decision-making and optimal control, the four infantry regiments fell directly under the division commander. However, two "combat commands" (depicted as brigade headquarters in figure one) offered the ability to task organize regiments for specific missions.[161] Gavin built this concept based on his experience in World War II and his vision of trends in technology and future conflict.

Once the communist threat emerged as preeminent during the Cold War, Gavin adjusted his ideas based on how he understood the Soviets. The way he expected the Soviets to progress technologically and engage locally shaped his views about the reorganization of U.S. Army forces. When he wrote about the Soviet threat, he admitted that the Soviets were difficult to define, and used Winston Churchill's famous quote, "Russia is a riddle, wrapped in a mystery inside an enigma."[162] However, he sought to outline the "substance of Soviet thinking" and what policies would drive Soviet application of their military capabilities.[163] To approach Soviet thinking, Gavin looked to Clausewitz, who had served with both Western European (Prussian) and Russian militaries and whose writing influenced the Soviet founding fathers, specifically Lenin.[164] Gavin thought that Clausewitz' *On War* was the "Rosetta Stone to Soviet military thinking."[165] The unmistakable link between war and politics that Clausewitz posited was a central theme in Communist theory, and Communists used violence to advance policy in ways the West

---

[159] Gavin, *Airborne Warfare*, 166-169.

[160] Ibid., 166.

[161] Ibid.

[162] Gavin, *War and Peace in the Space Age*, 180.

[163] Ibid.

[164] Ibid., 182.

[165] Ibid.

found difficult to reconcile with Western notions of war and peace that did not fit Communist thinking.[166]

Gavin also stressed the complete control that the Communist Party maintains over all military matters, to include exporting military equipment to satellite nations and Communist uprisings, all in the name of achieving victory over capitalist countries.[167] Gavin concluded that the Soviets, with their modern military power and missile and space advantage over the West, would carry on Lenin's teaching "by instigating and carrying out many types of local aggression" of many forms to advance the Communist position with respect to the capitalist Western world.[168] His understanding of the Soviet threat links directly to his belief in the need to maintain capability for limited wars, a capability he felt that the U.S. was neglecting in favor of strategic nuclear retaliation.

Communist actions in limited wars in Korea and Indochina demonstrated Gavin's belief in Communist intentions and he promoted greater readiness for limited conventional war in such theaters. Gavin wrote that the "real tragedy of Korea" was that the United States, with its scientific and industrial potential, failed to develop a "combat capability that would provide the technical margin of advantage that we needed in land warfare to win decisively and quickly."[169] He discussed Korea in terms of limited war, which was "limited in geographic area, in objectives and in the resources that the participating nations were willing to commit to the area."[170] He later refined his concept of limited war and suggested

---

[166] Gavin, *War and Peace in the Space Age*, 182-183. Gavin highlighted this point with a quote from a Congressional Committee on Un-American Activities, May 29, 1957. Dr. Frederick Schwarz testifying,

> You have to understand that their basic concept is that class war is a fact of being and that peace is the historical synthesis when communism defeats the remainder of the world and establishes world Communist dictatorship, which is peace. If you ask a true Communist to take a lie detector test and him if he wants peace, he would pass it with ease. He would look at you with a light in his eye and say he longs for peace. . . . Every act that contributes to the Communist conquest is a peaceful act. If they take a gun, they take a peaceful gun, containing a peaceful bullet, and kill you peacefully and put you in a peaceful grave. When the Chinese Communists murder millions, it is an act of peace. When the Russian tanks rolled into Budapest to butcher and destroy, it was glorious peace. Peace is wonderful and within their framework of ideology whatever helps their conquest is peaceful, good, and true.

[167] Ibid., 186-187, 189.

[168] Ibid., 198.

[169] Ibid., 123.

[170] Ibid., 125.

that "since a nuclear holocaust must be avoided, it follows that a primary objective of both sides in a limited war should be to keep such a war limited … in duration as well as in weapons used and area fought over."[171] His solution to such limited wars was to have on hand "superior means … to respond to the aggression, swiftly and severely."[172] Robert Osgood, writing in 1957 and using the same examples in Korea and Indochina, shared Gavin's conviction of the Communist threat and need for limited war readiness as follows:

> Assuming that the United States maintains an adequate capacity for total war and that the Communists continue to conduct a rational and cautious foreign policy, designed to gain their ends by indirection and limited ventures rather than by massive military assault, the chief function of our capacity for total war will be to keep war limited. ... However, the fulfillment of this function will not be sufficient for the purposes of containment unless it is accompanied by a ready capacity to resist lesser aggressions by limited war. Otherwise the Communists can confront us with the choice between total war, non-resistance, and ineffective resistance; and the results of that situation would probably be piecemeal Communist expansion, the paralysis of Western diplomacy, and the further disaffection of uncommitted peoples. Therefore, preparation for limited war is as vital to American security as preparation for total war. ... In developing a capacity for limited war we would be preparing to meet the most likely contingency; we would be maintaining the only credible military deterrent to Communist advances in the most vulnerable areas of the world.[173]

Gavin used the French experience at Dien Bien Phu to lend further clarity to his argument against the policy of massive retaliation and for conventional readiness. Planners at the Pentagon weighed several options to support the French, but the communists had offered another limited war that the United States was not prepared, technologically or intellectually, to join.[174] Gavin argued that with different defense spending priorities the United States could have had the means such as, "tactical nuclear missiles, sky cavalry, and increased assault airlift" that could "contribute decisively to that kind of an operation."[175] He rejected the assumption that readiness for total war meant readiness for a limited war, saying, "A thermo-

---

[171] Gavin, *Crisis Now*, 12.

[172] Gavin, *War and Peace in the Space Age*, 125.

[173] Robert Osgood, *Limited War, The Challenge to American Strategy* (Chicago: University of Chicago Press, 1957), 236-237.

[174] Gavin, *War and Peace in the Space Age*, 127.

[175] Ibid., 128.

nuclear equipped B-52 can contribute little more to the solution of a limited local war than a 155-mm gun can contribute to the apprehension of a traffic violator."[176] Finding technological solutions for limited wars occupied much of Gavin's time and intellect while his experience, observations, and testing shaped his ideas on optimal organizations to fight limited wars while maintaining total war capability.

Integrating his ideas on limited war, the Soviet threat, and the nuclear battlefield, Gavin considered and tested various requirements for organizing a force while in command of VII Corps. After several exercises, he "learned that the World War II type organizations, no matter how packaged, would not adapt themselves to nuclear tactics. The one exception was our armored divisions."[177] Gavin determined that the infantry division needed to reorganize from a linear defense model to an amorphous one, built into "small, widely dispersed battle groups, each one capable of sustained combat on its own, but not one ever offering a tactical nuclear target to the Soviets."[178] His description of "battle groups" suggested combined-arms building block organizations that did not easily align by size or equipment with existing battalions or regiments. These battle groups, dispersed for defensive operations, needed adequate mobility to rapidly transition to offensive operations.[179] He suggested several of these requirements in 1954 when he wrote: "Since dispersion – individual and unit – will characterize the defense, the greatest need of all will be for the means of concentrating rapidly in the area, and at the time, of decision."[180] These mutually supporting ideas of dispersion and rapid concentration clearly required mobility and control to execute, with firepower required for effectiveness.

The other organizational concept that Gavin wrote about extensively was the lack of a true cavalry arm. Gavin argued that General Walker's Eighth Army suffered much higher casualties early in

---

[176] Ibid., 128.

[177] Ibid., 137-139. The VII Corps force-on-force exercises "BATTLE MACE" and "BEARTRAP" followed staff planning exercises while Gavin was in command.

[178] Ibid., 138-139.

[179] Ibid., 139.

[180] Gavin, "Cavalry, and I Don't Mean Horses," 60.

the Korean War because they lacked cavalry with the mobility to conduct reconnaissance and screening missions forward of infantry and armored units.[181] He also lamented the lack of cavalry available to rapidly exploit success after the Inchon landing, cavalry that could also have warned of the Chinese divisions crossing the Yalu River.[182] While Gavin stopped short of publishing an ideal organization for the force, he offered the following suggestions for aircraft types and employment of sky cavalry:

> The first requirement is for a relatively light, easy to hand reconnaissance helicopter that can operate in pairs, with sufficient flexibility to gain information, preclude surprise, and handle enough fire to protect itself and get away. The next requirement is for support helicopters that would carry on the order of a dozen men, including hand-carried nuclear weapons. These men should have the capability of seizing tactical objectives and holding them for prolonged periods of time, short of sustained combat. The next requirement is for command helicopters that are equipped with sufficient communication gear to control effectively the forces described above. ... Logistical support air vehicles should be developed to perform the logistic function. Some will be the nature of flying cranes and others will be flying fuel tanks that would be used to refuel the forces described above after one force leap-frogged over the element being refueled.[183]

Gavin visualized a sky cavalry troop for each division, a full sky cavalry division for each corps, and a cavalry corps for a field army or theater headquarters.[184] He admitted that this amount of air mobility would not likely exist, but warned about the potential and danger of a force so equipped if the Soviets fielded a like organization.[185] Considering airborne divisions against the threat of air defense missiles and their limited mobility once inserted, Gavin recommended they reorganize to sky cavalry divisions while retaining their parachute delivery capability to retain flexibility of employment.[186] Having covered the formations he wrote most consistently about, it is worthwhile to consider other organizations.

As he considered division organizations, Gavin felt that the combat forces of the division needed to be reorganized "to enable the division to survive under the impact of nuclear weapons and react to win

---

[181] Ibid., 54.

[182] Ibid., 55.

[183] Gavin, "The Mobility Differential," 36.

[184] Ibid., 35.

[185] Ibid.

[186] Gavin, *War and Peace in the Space Age*, 271-272.

in tactical nuclear combat."[187] He believed the Soviets would employ tactical nuclear weapons so dispersion, as mentioned earlier, had to be adequate to preserve the division's fighting capability after a tactical nuclear strike. Maintaining capability meant each division needed enough combat power that suffering the loss of one element to a nuclear strike would not render the division ineffective. Gavin envisioned divisions organized around the battle groups he recommended following the VII Corps exercises in 1953.[188] Command and control for the battle groups fell to "combat commands" that would assume the "numerical designations, records, and histories" of regiments.[189] To further reduce vulnerability, divisions needed to push administrative functions to a higher level of command to maintain maximum mobility and flexibility in close battle since the WWII and Korean divisions were "burdened with truck trains and vast tonnages of supplies."[190] Using combat commands and reducing the logistics train size was consistent with the quadrilateral airborne division he recommended in 1947, but that division retained the infantry regiment as its primary building block. Furthermore, Gavin envisioned specialized division organizations, aside from the sky cavalry and airborne divisions, for mountainous and jungle terrain while the remainder of the divisions should have armored protection for greater effectiveness in a nuclear environment.[191] Gavin was one of many officers with organizational concepts, but his rank, experience, and outspoken voice placed several of his concepts near the forefront of the ongoing debate.

Gavin's position as the Army Assistant Chief of Staff for Operations (G-3) under General Ridgway placed him in an important role during General Ridgway's search for divisions that were "more

---

[187] Ibid., 270-271.

[188] Ibid., 139.

[189] James M. Gavin, "New Divisional Organizations," *Army-Navy-Air Force Register* 76, no. 3923 (February 12, 1955): 1.

[190] Gavin, *War and Peace in the Space Age,* 270-271.

[191] Ibid.

mobile, more flexible, and less vulnerable to atomic attack."[192] While his influence on Ridgway's thought

process remains unknown, the concepts outlined in *Airborne Warfare* and those he tested with VII Corps

aligned with Ridgway's objectives for reorganization given to Army Field Forces in April 1954 to

explore: "(1) greater combat manpower ratios; (2) greater combat to support unit ratios; (3) greater

flexibility and greater mobility in combat units; [and] (4) maximum use of technological

improvements."[193] Army Field Forces combined efforts with the Command and General Staff College to

develop the Atomic Field Army "ATFA-1" recommendation in September 1954 (see figure two

below).[194] Initial testing brought recommendations from the field to adjust the organization that resulted

in end strength around 17,000 troops, nearly the same as the organization it was to replace.[195]

---

[192] Wilson, *Maneuver and Firepower*, 264-265.

[193] Ibid., 265. Wilson outlined seven objectives that Ridgway tasked Army Field Forces to consider, the four listed above plus "(5) improvements in the Army's capability to sustain land combat; (6) development of tactical doctrine to support the changes; and (7) reorganization of the units by 1 January 1956."

[194] Ibid.

[195] Ibid., 269. Wilson lists post-Korean War infantry division authorized strength at 17,452 on page 252.

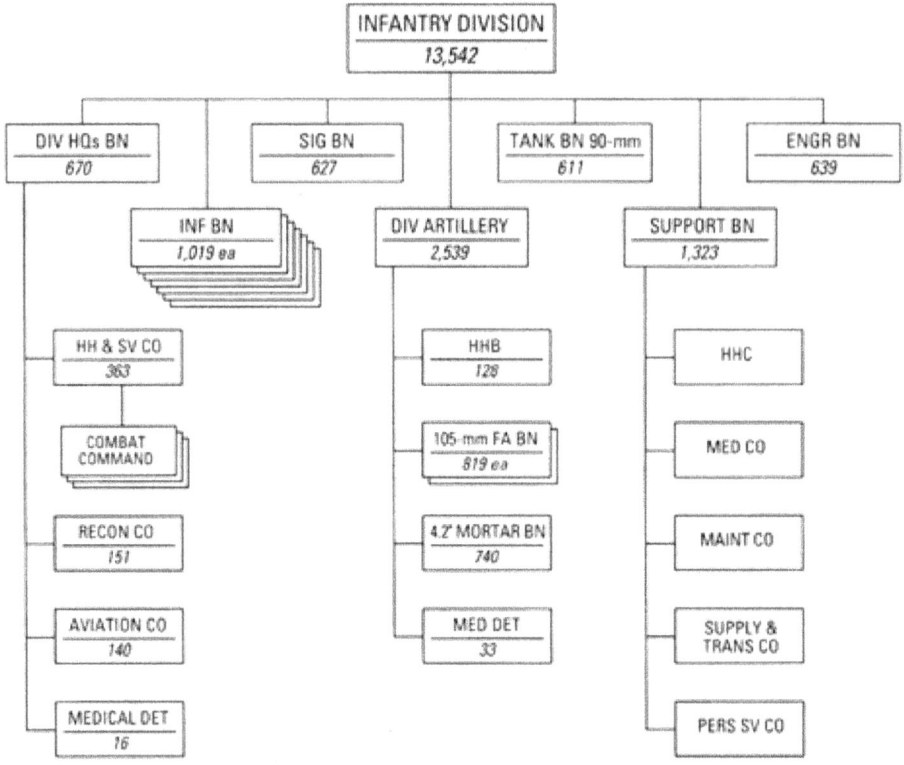

Figure 2: ATFA-1 Infantry Division Recommendation, September 1954.[196]

At a press conference in February 1955, Gavin discussed ongoing tests of the revised ATFA-1 divisional reorganization involving combat commands and battle groups.[197] He declined to offer specific details, but noted the divisions would fight in a "cellular rather than linear" fashion, and included "new development in communications, intelligence gathering, firepower, and above all mobility to keep from concentrating large numbers of men in one spot, and to avoid the old monolithic logistics line from a rear to a forward area."[198] Gavin's organizational concepts, then, grew from his experience, theory of future warfare, practical testing and exercises, and dialogue with Ridgway and other senior leaders.

---

[196] Ibid., 266. Wilson's diagram is labeled "Chart 26 – Atomic Field Army Infantry Division, 30 September 1954." This structure expanded to around 17,000 by December 1954 after test recommendations were implemented.

[197] Gavin, "New Divisional Organizations," 1.

[198] Ibid., 1, 21.

Section 3: Gavin's Concepts Realized in Division-level Organizations

General Ridgway's directive to Army Field Forces initiated several studies and tests of reorganization concepts (one of which was the aforementioned ATFA-1 concept). The Army War College submitted one such study, "Doctrinal and Organizational Concepts for Atomic-Nonatomic Army During the Period 1960-1970," in December 1955.[199] This report, with the short title "PENTANA," gained the attention of General Maxwell Taylor, Ridgway's successor as Chief of Staff of the Army, who approved the report, despite significant objections from across the Army, in June 1956 as a basis for future organizations.[200] Calling it the "pentomic" division, General Taylor selected his former unit, the 101st Airborne Division, to reorganize and start testing the PENTANA concepts in April 1956.[201] Taylor thought the pentomic organization fulfilled the need to produce leaner divisions (the ATFA-1 concepts recommended minimal reductions from standing organizations), offered capability on the nuclear and non-nuclear battlefield, gave the army a modern and attractive publicity, and supported the Eisenhower Administration's desire to reduce the Army's end strength.[202] With minor revisions, Continental Army Command published three tables of organization and equipment in 1956 for the pentomic divisions, Airborne, Infantry, and Armor (see figure 3).[203] For the infantry division, the pentomic reorganization, as visualized by Taylor, resulted in a reduction of nearly 4,000 troops.[204] Aside from the personnel reduction, the most significant change was the removal of a level of command between the division and the battle group.

---

[199] Wilson, *Maneuver and Firepower*, 270-271.

[200] Ibid., 271.

[201] Ibid., 274.

[202] Trauschweizer, *The Cold War U.S. Army*, 56.

[203] Wilson, *Maneuver and Firepower*, 274-280. Wilson includes charts for each of the three divisions, only the Infantry Division is used here as an example.

[204] Ibid., 277.

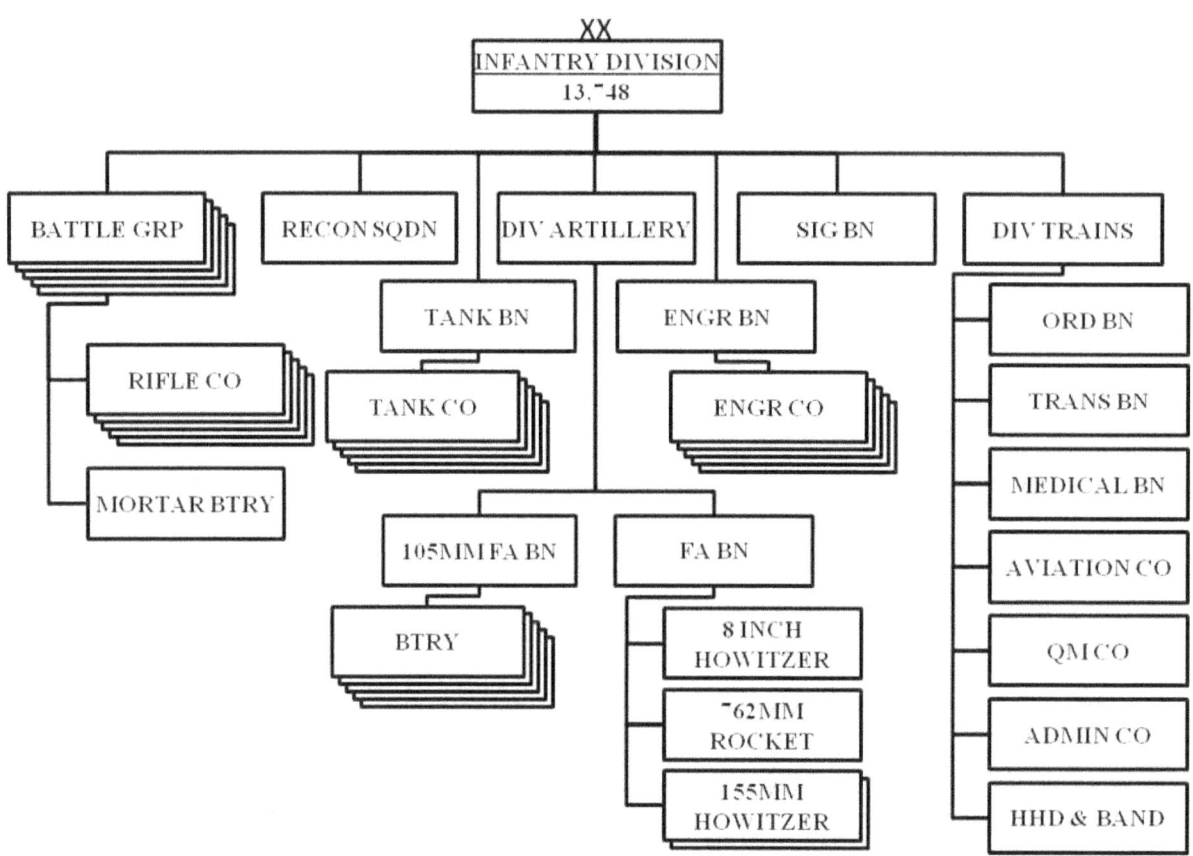

Figure 3: The Pentomic Infantry Division, 1956[205]

There were no combat commands, brigades, or regiments in the organization (see figure three for the

basic structure of the pentomic division) so a division commander directly controlled each of five infantry

battle groups plus a tank battalion, division artillery, a reconnaissance squadron, an engineer battalion,

signal battalion, and the division trains.

The most apparent link to Gavin's concepts in the pentomic division is its organization around the

battle group. The pentomic division had five battle groups under the division headquarters, and

supporting arms (artillery, armor, and engineers) each had five batteries or companies to create the self-

sufficient combined-arms battle groups Gavin envisioned. Missing from the pentomic division were the

---

[205] Ibid., 278. Wilson's original diagram was labeled "Chart 30 – Infantry Division (ROCID), 21 December 1956" and is reformatted here by the author for clarity.

combat commands he spoke about in 1955.[206] After his retirement in 1958, Gavin wrote that the pentomic division was "seriously lacking in missile fire power and adequate reconnaissance, both sky cavalry and drones … and more of its administrative personnel [should be] moved far to the rear."[207] During a 1975 interview, he described the pentomic division as a "mess" that was "grossly lacking in artillery."[208] Both these comments demonstrate Gavin's concept of firepower, clearly a concern with a division that fielded 4,000 fewer troops than its predecessor and intended to fight dispersed on the battlefield. However, by introducing tactical nuclear weapons into the pentomic division, test reports praised the "decisive combat power" offered by the nuclear weapons.[209] The pentomic division offered improved strategic mobility, with fewer personnel and less equipment, but tactical mobility was largely similar to Korean War-era divisions, albeit with fewer combat support troops. Bacevich argued that this lack of tactical mobility was due to the Army's politically motivated spending on missile development (43% of the FY57 research and development budget) to the detriment of aircraft and mechanization improvements (combined for 8.5% of the research and development budget).[210] Wilson and Trauschweizer both argued that the pentomic divisions were Taylor's short-term method to secure budget dollars for the Army because the Eisenhower administration did not support more a more conventional approach.[211] In all, while the pentomic reorganization coincided with Gavin's last years in service and included elements of some of his concepts, he clearly disagreed with the overall structure and it was not in line with his concepts of firepower, mobility, and control.

---

[206] Gavin, "New Divisional Organizations," 1.

[207] Gavin, *War and Peace in the Space Age*, 271.

[208] James M. Gavin, interview by Donald G. Andrews and Charles H. Ferguson, Cambridge, MA, May 29, 1975, transcript, Senior Officers Debriefing Program, U.S. Army Military History Institute, Carlisle Barracks, PA, 45.

[209] Wilson, *Maneuver and Firepower*, 282.

[210] Bacevich, *The Pentomic Era*, 99-100, 103. Bacevich used a quote from General Gavin to Congress in 1957 to highlight the spending disparity.

[211] Wilson, *Maneuver and Firepower*, 286. Trauschweizer, *The Cold War U.S. Army*, 56.

The organization that epitomized Gavin's concepts and occupied much of his attention was what he called sky cavalry. Gavin consistently argued for improved mobility, both land and air, and increased cavalry capability. His favored approach was sky cavalry. In addition to advocating sky cavalry concepts and continuing the public and professional debate about mobility, particularly through the air, Gavin also placed key personnel into positions to promote future air mobility development. One of the most influential people Gavin placed was then Major General Hamilton Howze, an armor officer, who Gavin selected in 1956 as the G-3 Director of Army Aviation.[212] Weinert noted that Howze's appointment, and the creation of the "Directorate of Army Aviation," had a "profound effect" on the advancement of army aviation capabilities "and the introduction of airmobility into combat operations."[213] General Howze's most prominent contribution was as chair of the 1962 Tactical Mobility Requirements Board (nicknamed the Howze Board), formed in response to Secretary of Defense Robert McNamara's request to reconsider the Army aviation program.[214] The Howze Board "recommended sweeping changes in the Army's aviation program and force structure based on air assault divisions and air cavalry combat brigades equipped with armed helicopters, fixed-wing fire support, and other aircraft."[215] Another key air mobility advocate was Lieutenant General John J. Tolson, who as a Lieutenant Colonel was Gavin's Director of Doctrine and Combat Development in the Department of the Army G-3 shop in the mid-1950s.[216] Gavin worked through the Army G-1 and the Commandant of the Infantry School to assign Tolson to "develop tactical doctrine for the combat employment of helicopters."[217] Tolson's significant contribution to airmobility continued as he served as the assistant commandant of the aviation school, commander of the 1st Cavalry Division (Airmobile) during Vietnam, and later commanding general of the XVIII Airborne

---

[212] Stockfisch, "Howze Board," 9. Gavin's original title for Howze was "Chief of the G-3 Aviation Section," but it was a staff position, later recognized as the Director of Army Aviation.

[213] Weinert, *A History of Army Aviation*, 269.

[214] Stockfisch, "Howze Board," 1.

[215] Ibid., x.

[216] Tolson, *Airmobility*, 4.

[217] Ibid., 4-5.

Corps.[218] While Howze and Tolson entered the aviation community as established officers, Gavin also helped to change an Army policy that "required young lieutenants to hold tactical field assignments before attending flight school" to allow West Point graduates to enter flight school before they were overage.[219] Thus by bringing in established senior officers and creating greater opportunity for junior officers, Gavin supported the perceived legitimacy of the aviation branch and helped shape future development.

While helping place key individuals to further air mobility development, Gavin also promoted air mobility concepts in public forums and with official guidance. Richard Weinert, a Department of the Army Historian, credited Gavin's "Cavalry, and I Don't Mean Horses" article, published in 1954 in *Harper's Magazine* as having a significant "impact on military thinking" in the mid-1950s.[220] In his official capacity, Gavin directed that Army Field Forces, during their 1955 SAGE BRUSH exercise, "develop the application of airlift by helicopter" by combat arms units.[221] He also tasked his G-3 section to "design new hypothetical cavalry organizations around the potential of the helicopter" in mid-1954.[222] Gavin also published a number of articles in various journals in the mid-1950s, many of which, as noted earlier, advocate air mobility. Gavin's influence continued after his retirement, both with public articles and through some of his key advocates. He wrote the following comments to the 1962 Howze Board participants which closed the section outlining mobility requirements in the board's final report:

> If there is one thing that stands out clearly in all recorded history of man's military endeavors, it is that innovation is essential to survival and is usually decisive in battle – Regardless of the weapons system employed, but assuming it is employed with reasonable intelligence and direction, the final criterion of effectiveness is the product of both firepower and mobility. These

---

[218] Bergerson, *Army Gets an Air Force*, 105.

[219] Rosen, *Winning the Next War*, 89. Rosen cited an interview with LTG Williams, Howze's predecessor at Aviation Branch, who approached Gavin with the problem in an attempt to increase the branch's legitimacy in the service. Gavin bypassed the G-1 and went directly to the Chief of Staff of the Army, Maxwell Taylor, for resolution.

[220] Richard P. Weinert, Jr., *A History of Army Aviation – 1950-1962,* TRADOC Historical Monograph Series (Fort Monroe, VA: U.S. Army Training and Doctrine Command (TRADOC), 1991), 181.

[221] Ibid., 183.

[222] Tolson, *Airmobility*, 4-5.

may have exponential values, and in fact, the mobility part usually does. It is in a thorough exploration of the field of mobility, and the application of the knowledge gained, that we will find the greatest possibility for innovation in the future. … The demand for this form of mobility may be quite staggering … but if the Soviets develop their forces along these lines and match them with tactical nuclear firepower, they will not only defeat us in all guerrilla action but drive us like chaff before the wind in general conflagration.[223]

Aside from references to Gavin in the board's final report, Dr. Jacob Stockfisch, a member of the advisory panel to the board, noted Gavin's sky cavalry concept as one of the three "roots" of the board's formation and direction.[224] His influence was clearly seen in the personnel and requirements facing the Howze Board, Gavin's concepts also shaped the board's research and are evident in the board's recommendations.

The Howze Board recommended a vast increase in combat aviation assets and the formation of specialized units to exploit air mobility. The board considered various implementation options, but recommended a balanced program that included designation and conversion of specific airmobile units and retention of the remainder of the current (1962) force structure with added organic aviation capability and establishment of corps-level aviation for flexible application.[225] The recommended structure resulted in "at the end of six years, eleven augmented ROAD divisions, five operational air assault divisions, three air cavalry combat brigades, strengthened armored cavalry regiments, and provisions for increasing the mobility of other combat units as well as the rapidity and responsiveness of their logistic support."[226] This broad recommendation for a balanced force of airmobile and existing organizations was a concept that Gavin valued after his experience with VII Corps. Writing to Dr. Vannevar Bush in May 1954, he noted that he was "not at all satisfied with a cavalry that would depend for its mobility entirely on an air vehicle" and agreed that a mix of heavy and light cavalry, and air-supplied light forces proved to be

---

[223] U.S. Department of the Army, *U.S. Army Tactical Mobility Requirements Board: Final Report* (Fort Monroe, VA: Continental Army Command, 20 August 1962), 16-17, under "Combined Arms Research Library Digital Library" http://cgsc.contentdm.oclc.org/cdm/ref/collection/p4013coll11/id/1689 (accessed August 14, 2012).

[224] Stockfisch, "Howze Board," 30. Dr. Stockfisch is identified as a member of the advisory panel on page ix of the *Tactical Mobility Requirements Board: Final Report*.

[225] U.S. Army, *Tactical Mobility Requirements Board: Final Report*, 95.

[226] Ibid., 95.

promising concepts.[227] Gavin also made this force mix evident during testimony to the Senate

Appropriations Committee in 1957 as he outlined the challenges and benefits of air mobility facing Army

research and development efforts while stressing the importance of continued development of ground

mobility.[228] In highlighting the need for balance, he also warned against bias toward one specific form of

warfare or tactic, noting that "the Army has its partisans … who would emphasize air mobility at the

expense of everything else, while others would put [the Army's] emphasis on sustained combat and heavy

armored equipment."[229] Therefore, while Gavin was a strong advocate of air mobility and sky cavalry, he

was not blind to the need for a balanced force and development of modern equipment for conventional

and air mobile forces. As such, the overall concept of the board's recommendation aligned with trends he

predicted and advocated during his service.

While the broad, balanced recommendation avoided over-reliance on air mobility, the board's

most noteworthy recommendation was the air assault division as shown below.

---

[227] James Gavin to Vannevar Bush, May 3, 1954, Vannevar Bush Papers, General Correspondence: Box 42, Manuscript Division, Library of Congress, Washington, D.C.

[228] Senate Committee on Appropriations. *Department of Defense Appropriations for 1958: Hearings before the Subcommittee on H.R. 7665.* 85th Cong., 1st Sess., 1957, 869-872, 881.

[229] Gavin, *War and Peace in the Space Age*, 248. This is a small part of his larger argument against the policy of Massive Retaliation as well, the reliance on a single weapon system and tactic to the detriment of nearly all others.

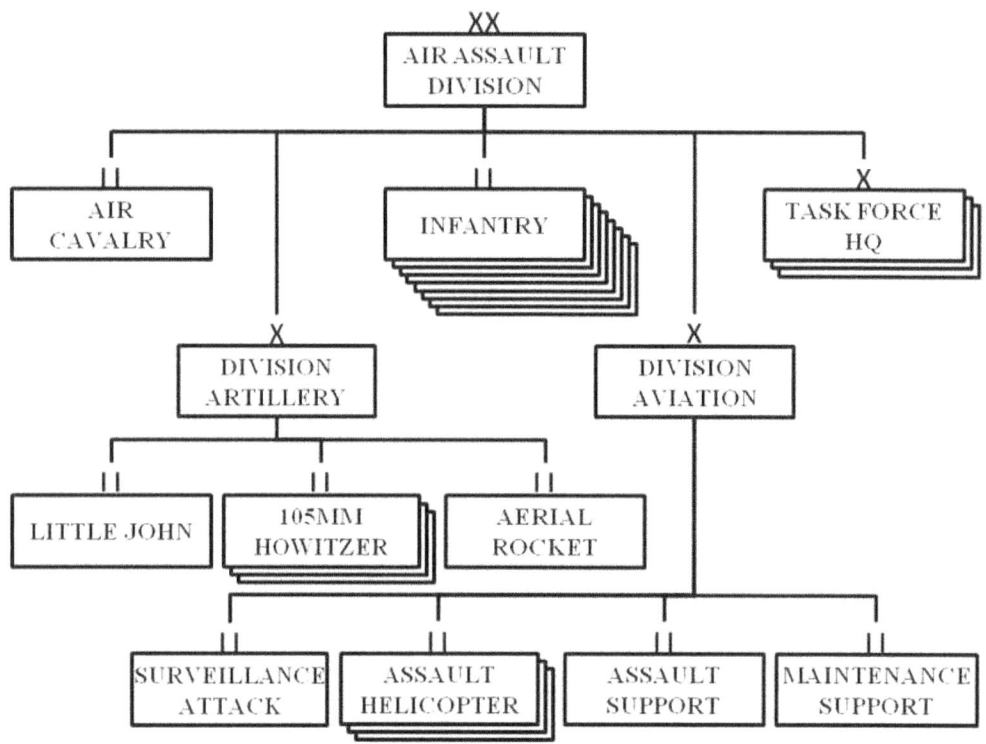

Figure 4: Howze Board's Recommended Air Assault Division[230]

The air assault division retained the triangular design (three major subordinate units, shown as the

brigade-level task force headquarters) adopted following the pentomic experiment (see figure four above),

as opposed to the quadrilateral organization Gavin recommended in 1947 (figure one), and was built

around eight infantry battalions with three brigade-level task force headquarters elements. The mix of

rocket, atomic, and conventional fire support in the division artillery brigade echo Gavin's desire for

improved fire support that included rocket and atomic capability. In keeping with Gavin's concepts, the

combat formations in the division remained as light as possible and consolidated combat support and

administrative elements outside of the combat arms units to maximize tactical air mobility of the combat

forces.[231] The recommended air assault division also enjoyed significant reduction in strategic airlift over

its counterpart divisions and needed only 75 percent of the airlift required to deploy an airborne division

---

[230] U.S. Army, *Tactical Mobility Requirements Board: Final Report*, 36. The original diagram was labeled "Figure I. The Air Assault Division" and is reformatted here by the author for clarity and to more closely resemble Wilson's diagrams (figures two and three).

[231] Ibid., 37-38.

and less than 50 percent of the infantry division's requirement.[232] While the board's recommended air assault division eschewed the quadrilateral organization and battle group sub-units Gavin wrote about, the unit clearly reflected elements of his organizational concepts.

While the air assault divisional organization showed elements of Gavin's concepts, the advantages outlined in the board's recommendation highlight how much Gavin's ideas influenced military thought at the time. General Howze's report lists eight "benefits to be derived" from acceptance of the board's recommendation, Gavin's writings foreshadowed each advantage as noted in the chart below.[233]

---

[232] Ibid., 39.

[233] Ibid., 14-15.

Howze Board Advantage	Foreshadowed by Gavin in:
The [recommended] Army will have an unusual flexibility of response to any of the likely demands for the application of land combat power, and a much improved effectiveness in execution.	Mar-Apr 1955 : "Arms Vigilance for Peace" Nov 1955: "We Can Solve Our Tech. Difficulties" 1957: Testimony to Senate Committee 1958: *War and Peace in the Space Age* (226-227)
- Better deployability of airmobile forces will permit faster reaction by the general reserve.	Jan 1948: "Future of Armor" Apr 1954 : "Cavalry, and I Don't Mean Horses" Mar 1955: "Interview with General Gavin" Nov 1955: "We Can Solve Our Tech. Difficulties" 1957: Testimony to Senate Committee 1958 : *War and Peace in the Space Age* (226, 283-284)
- Improved tactical mobility will provide the best foreseeable chance of coping with the largely unknown contingencies of the land battle in an atomic war.	1947: *Airborne Warfare* (140, 170) Nov 1950: "Tactical Use of the Atomic Bomb" Apr 1954: "Cavalry, and I Don't Mean Horses" Feb 1955: "New Divisional Organizations" Mar 1955: "Interview with General Gavin" Mar-Apr 1955: "Arms Vigilance for Peace" Nov 1955: "We Can Solve Our Tech. Difficulties" 1958: *War and Peace in the Space Age* (226)
- Greater mobility will improve the chances of success of the detection, screening and delay missions charged to the cavalry regiments which, in Germany, form the forward fringes of the "shield."	1947: *Airborne Warfare* (171) Apr 1954: "Cavalry, and I Don't Mean Horses" 1958: *War and Peace in the Space Age* (227-228)
- A highly mobile counterattack reserve, strong in anti-tank weapons, will, in Europe, serve as a most valuable counter to strong Soviet armored thrusts.	1947: *Airborne Warfare* (151, 174) Jan 1948: "Future of Armor" Apr 1954: "Cavalry, and I Don't Mean Horses" 1958: *War and Peace in the Space Age* (218, 276-277)
- Airmobile US units will provide the most effective augmentation to friendly indigenous forces fighting Communist armies in Southeast Asia or Korea, not only by reason of their freedom from local limitations to surface transportation but also because their extreme mobility will permit a flexibility of employment much to be desired, perhaps as a counterattack reserve or as a blocking or enveloping force.	Apr 1954: "Cavalry, and I Don't Mean Horses" Feb 1955: "New Divisional Organizations" Mar-Apr 1955: "Arms Vigilance for Peace" 1958: *War and Peace in the Space Age* (110-111, 124-125, 127-129, 218, 227, 278-279)
- Whatever the difficulties of detection and identification, airmobile forces have the best chance of surprising and eradicating guerrilla forces, and at the same time stand to suffer fewer losses due to the ambush of combat and supply columns.	Feb 1955: "New Divisional Organizations" Mar 1955: "Interview with General Gavin" 1958: *War and Peace in the Space Age* (270-271) **All these refer to discussions about reducing the vulnerable logistics tail via air mobility

Table 1: Parallels between Gavin's writings and Howze Board Advantages[234]

---

[234] Ibid., 14-15. The board's advantages are quoted directly with revisions only for spelling.

As shown above, Gavin predicted the benefits of improved tactical and strategic air mobility by considering possible forms of future warfare and the potential of future advances in various type aircraft for use in combat for long- and short-range transport, attack, and logistics in both conventional and atomic wars. After the Howze Board delivered its results in August 1962, Gavin's June 1963 article "The Mobility Differential" mirrors, in a broad sense, nearly all the recommendations of the report, to include the force mix of air cavalry units to conventional units, the types and use of various helicopters, and employment against conventional or guerrilla threats.[235] While the Howze Board's report remained classified, Gavin's article, presumably informed by the board's activities and conclusions, served to keep the air cavalry concept in the professional and public discussion about means in war.

The Howze Board's recommendations led quickly to the formation of a test airmobile division and ultimately to the adoption of air assault tactics and organizations in the Army in the mid-1960s. This process is well documented in a number of books, many of which credit Gavin with the genesis of the air cavalry concept.[236] The purpose here was specifically to consider Gavin's contributions to the effort. Considering the various reorganization and modernization programs during and shortly after Gavin's post-WWII career, the concepts and technologies that he consistently advocated were largely adopted, in some form or another, into organizations in the Army. From the ill-fated Pentomic Division of the late 1950s to the air cavalry that was the signature force of the Vietnam War, Gavin's concepts and influence shaped military thought and modernization efforts for over a decade.

---

[235] Gavin, "The Mobility Differential," 34-36.

[236] Books that cover the development of air cavalry and the adoption of air assault forces and their employment in Vietnam include the following: Bergerson's *The Army Gets an Air Force*, Cheng's *Air Mobility*, House's *Combined Arms Warfare in the Twentieth Century*, Galvin's *Air Assault: The Development of Airmobile Warfare*, Mahnken's *Technology and the American Way of War Since 1945*, Rosen's *Winning the Next War, Innovation and the Modern Military*, Tolson's *Airmobility 1961-1971*, Trauschweizer's *The Cold War U.S. Army: Building Deterrence for Limited War*, and Wilson's *Maneuver and Firepower: The Evolution of Divisions and Separate Brigades*.

Conclusion

While Gavin's views were not wholly unique when considered against fellow American thinkers following World War II and Korea, his influential position and comprehensive writings regarding aspects of conflict from tactics to strategy and policy solidify his position as an important military theorist. This monograph approached Gavin as a theorist and explored his influence as the Army transitioned from World War II to the Cold War. Gavin's theory of future warfare required an army with capability in atomic and non-atomic warfare and he recognized the need for readiness for both limited peripheral wars and general war. His theory shaped his vision of the functions, organizations, and technology required to succeed in future conflicts. Gavin organized much of his writing around the concepts of mobility, firepower, and control that he felt were critical for future warfare. His influence shaped development of tactical nuclear weapons, missiles, air mobility, and organizational transformation following World War II and into the Cold War.

Gavin's 1947 book, *Airborne Warfare*, introduced his vision of future general warfare while suggesting the dispersion and mobility required for warfare in an atomic environment. He outlined technological needs in firepower, communications, and tactical mobility and suggested organizational concepts to modernize the force. The concepts of air mobility and firepower continued in a series of articles in the late 1940s as Gavin argued for ground warfare capability in the face of dominant research, development, and funding focused on strategic atomic bombing.

The Korean War proved that ground combat was still relevant and Gavin was one of the most prominent officers suggesting that the Army should develop tactical nuclear weapons as an alternative to the increasingly large strategic bombs and bombers under development in the early 1950s. This focus stemmed from his understanding of the need for increased firepower for tactical commanders, his struggle to integrate decisive atomic technology into the Army, and his posting as a member of the Weapons System Evaluation Group. His involvement in the research and development community also resulted in his advocacy of missile technology as another form of firepower to extend the reach of tactical commanders into the depth of the future battlefield he envisioned.

In the mid-1950s, with many of his firepower concepts in development, Gavin returned to the Pentagon with refined concepts of capability gaps in the Army. He saw the lack of tactical and strategic mobility as a critical shortfall that hindered cavalry-type missions and projection of ground combat power. He also refined his vision of future atomic warfare and expanded his ideas about the need to have readiness for limited peripheral wars, with Korea as his primary evidence. He outlined his concepts for a more mobile force capable of fighting limited or general warfare on an atomic or non-atomic battlefield in a series of articles, interviews, and testimony to Congress. Following his retirement in 1958, Gavin consolidated his theory of future warfare, his view of the strategic context, and his concepts of mobility, firepower, and control into his book, *War and Peace in the Space Age*. In this book, like several of his earlier articles, he advocated reconsideration of national defense policies weighted towards strategic bombing and general war.

Gavin's theory of future warfare, his understanding of the Soviet threat, and his concepts of firepower, mobility, and control informed his model of how the Army should organize for future warfare. He envisioned flexible division organizations, capable of fighting dispersed over significant depth, enabled by superior air and ground mobility to deliver firepower adequate prevail on future battlefields. He supported General Ridgway's reorganizational concepts, but despite conceptual similarities with the eventual pentomic reorganization under General Taylor he recognized the pentomic division as a flawed organization that lacked adequate firepower and control.

The organization that epitomized Gavin's concepts was the air mobile division that developed from his sky cavalry concept. Gavin's advocacy for the air mobility concept and his specific actions to advance personnel and positions to build and refine sky cavalry and air mobility capabilities were key factors in the eventual development and acceptance of the airmobile division. Gavin clearly influenced military thought about air mobility as the recommendations by the 1962 Tactical Mobility Requirements Board, known as the Howze Board, follow many of the themes Gavin wrote about since the late 1940s (see Table 1). While airmobile divisions and sky cavalry would likely have emerged without Gavin, his influence clearly advanced the ideas and shaped the form of the organizations.

49

This monograph maintained a narrow focus on Gavin's theories and concepts through his writings, and interviews, and considered his influence on the Army's adaptation to the Cold War environment. Further research could track Gavin's concepts through Army doctrine, specifically FM 100-5, to investigate whether or when his concepts gained primacy in doctrine. Likewise, a parallel effort could identify other influential officers of the era, such as Generals Ridgway and Taylor, to consider where the three officers shared or differed on theories and approaches to adaptation. A similar study could follow an officer or group from the generation leading into Vietnam to see if the theory of future warfare, concept of dual-role capability for limited war or general war, and the concepts of mobility, firepower, and control gained acceptance or were rejected and replaced with new theories and concepts as the the Army found itself increasingly engaged in Vietnam. Gavin's ideas on air mobile cavalry remain relevant, and another vein of research may be the progression of air-transportable light armored vehicles from the M113 through the Stryker, the doctrine for their employment, and their use in combat from Vietnam through Iraq and Afghanistan.

Considering General Gavin's struggle with combat realities, emerging technologies, and uncertain threats is valuable to today's military officers. His method of developing a theory of future warfare from which he organized recognizable concepts and recommendations demonstrates a way that military professionals can stay relevant and engaged in the national defense discussion. Likewise his ability to articulate arguments and willingness to publish relevant and potentially controversial articles and books highlight the need for members of the military to capture their combat experience, measure its relevance against a concept of future conflict, and continue the dialogue about the form and functions our military needs to succeed in future warfare.

Bibliography

Bacevich, A.J. *The Pentomic Era.* Washington DC: National Defense University Press, 1986.

Bergerson, Frederic A. *The Army Gets an Air Force: Tactics of Insurgent Bureaucratic Politics.* Baltimore, MD: The Johns Hopkins University Press, 1980.

Biggs, Bradley. *Gavin.* Hamden, CT: Archon Books, 1980.

Booth, T. Michael, and Duncan Spencer. *Paratrooper: The Life of Gen. James M. Gavin.* New York, NY: Simon & Schuster, 1994.

Carland, John M. *How We Got There: Air Assault and the Emergence of the 1st Cavalry Division (Airmobile), 1950-1965.* The Land Warfare Papers, No 42, Arlington, VA: Association of the United States Army, May 2003.

Cheng, Christopher C.S. *Air Mobility: The Development of a Doctrine.* Westport, CT: Praeger Publishers, 1994.

Davis II, Robert T. *The Challenge of Adaptation: The US Army in the Aftermath of Conflict, 1953-2000.* The Long War Series, OP 27, Fort Leavenworth, KS: Combat Studies Institute Press, 2008.

Doughty, Robert A. *The Evolution of US Army Tactical Doctrine 1946-1976.* Leavenworth Papers, No. 1, Fort Leavenworth, KS: Combat Studies Institute Press, 1979.

Galvin, John R. *Air Assault: The Development of Airmobile Warfare.* New York, NY: Hawthorn Books, Inc., 1969.

Gavin, James M. *Airborne Warfare.* Washington DC: Infantry Journal Press, 1947.

—. "Arms Vigilance for Peace." *Ordnance* 39, no. 209 (March-April 1955): 716-719.

—. "Cavalry, and I Don't Mean Horses." *Harper's Magazine* (Harper & Brothers), April 1954: 54-61.

—. *Crisis Now.* New York, NY: Random House, 1968.

—. "New Divisional Organizations." *Army-Navy-Air Force Register* 76, no. 3923 (February 1955): 1,21.

—. *On to Berlin.* New York, NY: The Viking Press, 1978.

—., interview by Donald G. Andrews and Charles H. Ferguson. *Senior Officers Debriefing Program* Carlisle Barracks, PA: U.S. Army Military History Insitute, (May 29, 1975).

—. "The Future of Airborne Operations." *Military Review* XXVII, no. 9 (December 1947): 3-8.

—. "The Future of Armor." *Infantry Journal* LXII, no. 1 (January 1948): 7-11.

—. "The Mobility Differential." *Army* 13, no. 11 (June 1963): 34-36.

—. "The Tactical Use of the Atomic Bomb." *Combat Forces Journal* 1, no. 4 (November 1950): 9-11.

—. *War and Peace in the Space Age.* New York, NY: Harper & Brothers, 1958.

—. "We Can Solve Our Technical Difficulties." *Army Combat Forces Journal*, November 1955: 64-65.

House, Jonathan M. *Combined Arms Warfare in the Twentieth Century.* Lawrence, KS: University Press of Kansas, 2001.

Jussel, Paul C. *Intimidating the World: The United States Atomic Army, 1956-1960.* PhD Dissertation, The Ohio State University, 2004.

Linn, Brian McAllister. *The Echo of Battle: The Army's Way of War.* Cambridge, MA: Harvard University Press, 2007.

Lofaro, Guy A. *Gavin, James Maurice.* Vols. 2: D-K, in *Encyclopedia of World War II: A Political, Social, and Military History*, edited by Spencer C. Tucker (et. al), 572. Santa Barbara, CA: ABC-Clio, 2005.

Mahnken, Thomas G. *Technology and the American Way of War.* New York, NY: Columbia University Press, 2008.

Mataxis, Theodore C. *Nuclear Tactics, Weapons, and Firepower in the Pentomic Division, Battle Group, and Company.* Harrisburg, PA: The Military Service Publishing Company, 1958.

Ney, Virgil. *Evolution of the U.S. Army Division: 1939-1968.* Combat Operations Research Group Memorandum CORG-M-365., Fort Belvoir, VA: Technical Operations, Inc.,Combat Operations Research Group for U.S. Army Combat Developments Command, January 1969.

Osgood, Robert Endicott. *Limited War: The Challenge to American Strategy.* Chicago, IL: The University of Chicago Press, 1957.

Reinhardt, G. C., and W. R. Kintner. *Atomic Weapons in Land Combat.* Harrisburg, PA: The Military Service Publishing Company, 1953.

Ridgway, Matthew B. *Soldier: The Memoirs of Matthew B. Ridgway.* New York, NY: Harper & Brothers, 1956.

Rosen, Stephen Peter. *Winning the Next War: Innovation and the Modern Military.* New York, NY: Cornell University Press, 1991.

Stockfisch, Jacob A. *The 1962 Howze Board and Army Combat Developments.* Santa Monica, CA: RAND, 1994.

Taylor, Maxwell D. *The Uncertain Trumpet.* New York, NY: Harper & Brothers, 1960.

Tolson, John J. *Airmobility: 1961-1971.* Department of the Army Vietnam Studies Series. Washington, D.C.: Government Printing Office, 1973.

Trauschweizer, Ingo. *The Cold War U.S. Army: Building Deterrence for Limited War.* Lawrence, KS: University Press of Kansas, 2008.

U.S. Congress. Senate. Committee on Appropriations. *Department of Defense Appropriations for 1958: Hearings before the Subcommittee on H.R. 7665.* 85th Cong., 1st Sess., 1957.

U.S. Department of the Army. *Tactical Mobility Requirements Board: Final Report.* Fort Monroe, VA: U.S. Continental Army Command, 1962.

Weigley, Russell Frank. *History of the United States Army.* Bloomington, IN: Indiana University Press, 1984.

—. *The American Way of War: A History of United States Military Strategy and Policy.* Bloomington, IN: Indiana University Press, 1977.

Weinert, Richard P. Jr. *A History of Army Aviation - 1950-1962.* TRADOC Historical Monograph Series. Fort Monroe, VA: U.S. Army Training and Doctrine Command (TRADOC), 1991.

White, Theodore H. "An Interview with General Gavin ... Tomorrow's Battlefield." *Army Combat Forces Journal*, March 1955: 20-23.

Wilson, John B. *Maneuver and Firepower: The Evolution of Divisions and Separate Brigades.* Washington, D.C.: Center of Military History, United States Army, 1998.